ANXIETY AND DEPRESSION IN TEENS

DEVELOP MINDFULNESS STRATEGIES AND COPING SKILLS TO MANAGE EMOTIONS, CONTROL YOUR THOUGHTS, AND BOOST CONFIDENCE

GRACE TAYLOR

© **Copyright 2023 - All rights reserved.**

The content contained within this book may not be reproduced, duplicated or transmitted without direct written permission from the author or the publisher.

Under no circumstances will any blame or legal responsibility be held against the publisher, or author, for any damages, reparation, or monetary loss due to the information contained within this book, either directly or indirectly.

Legal Notice:

This book is copyright protected. It is only for personal use. You cannot amend, distribute, sell, use, quote or paraphrase any part, or the content within this book, without the consent of the author or publisher.

Disclaimer Notice:

Please note the information contained within this document is for educational and entertainment purposes only. All effort has been executed to present accurate, up to date, reliable, complete information. No warranties of any kind are declared or implied. Readers acknowledge that the author is not engaged in the rendering of legal, financial, medical or professional advice. The content within this book has been derived from various sources. Please consult a licensed professional before attempting any techniques outlined in this book.

By reading this document, the reader agrees that under no circumstances is the author responsible for any losses, direct or indirect, that are incurred as a result of the use of the information contained within this document, including, but not limited to, errors, omissions, or inaccuracies.

CONTENTS

Introduction   7

1. WHAT DOES ANXIETY LOOK LIKE?   13
   Anxiety: First Things First   14
   Recognizing Anxiety: Common Symptoms   18
   Why Is It Happening, and How Do I Get It to Stop?   23
   Jayden's Story   27

2. TYPES OF ANXIETY DISORDERS AND INDICATORS   31
   What Is an Anxiety Disorder?   32
   A Note About Self-Diagnosing   33
   Types of Anxiety Disorders   36
   Indicators of Anxiety Disorders   44

3. PANIC ATTACKS VS. ANXIETY ATTACKS–DIFFERENCES AND COPING STRATEGIES   59
   Panic vs. Anxiety   60
   What to Do When You're Having an Attack   67
   Neal's Story   72
   First-Aid Kit   74

4. WHAT DOES DEPRESSION LOOK LIKE?   77
   Depression Is…   79
   Depression: What to Expect   83
   Why Is This Happening, and How Do I Get It to Stop?   87
   Clinical Confirmation   91

5. COMMON MISCONCEPTIONS ABOUT
   ANXIETY AND DEPRESSION   97
   Myth 1: Teenagers Don't Actually Suffer
   From Depression and Anxiety, They Just
   Feel Down Sometimes   98
   Myth 2: Treatment for Anxiety and
   Depression Is Easily Accessible   98
   Myth 3: Depression Is Caused by an
   Unstable Family   99
   Myth 4: If You Have Anxiety, You Will
   Fall Apart and Won't Be Able To Achieve
   Success   99
   Myth 5: All Teenagers Experience
   Depression Sometime During
   Adolescence. It Is Just a Phase.   101
   Myth 6: Technology Causes Depression
   and Anxiety   101
   Myth 7: She's Not Depressed/Anxious,
   She's Just Lazy.   102
   Myth 8: All Anxiety Is Bad   103
   Myth 9: You Can Fix Your Anxiety With
   Some Coping Strategies   104
   Myth 10: Your Parents Can Make Your
   Anxiety Go Away, If They Would Just…   104
   Myth 11: You Just Have to Face Your
   Fears!   105
   Myth 12: You're Just Manipulating Your
   Parents   105
   Myth 13: Having Anxiety or Depression
   Is Hopeless   106

6. TAKING CONTROL–COGNITIVE
   BEHAVIORAL THERAPY   107
   What is Cognitive Behavioral Therapy?   108
   How Does CBT Help With Anxiety and
   Depression?   112
   CBT: Battling Cognitive Distortions With
   Cognitive Interventions   118

CBT in Action	124

7. **TAKING CONTROL–THE POWER OF YOUR THOUGHTS** — 127
   Mindset Matters: Fixed vs. Growth — 128
   The Power of a Growth Mindset — 130
   Your Thoughts Influence Your Surroundings — 133
   Hacks to Trick Your Body Into Happiness — 134
   Kamrin's Story — 140

8. **TAKING CONTROL–MANAGING AND MASTERING DAILY TRIGGERS** — 143
   Understanding and Identifying Triggers — 144
   Coping Skills and Management Methods — 151

9. **TAKING CONTROL–DEVELOPING YOUR STRENGTHS** — 159
   Fighting Anxiety With Action — 160
   Hobbies and Skills to Cope With Anxiety — 161
   Band-Aid Solutions — 165

10. **TAKING CONTROL–YOU'RE NOT ALONE** — 169
    Online Therapy — 171
    Group Counseling Sessions — 171
    Meditation and Mental Health Apps — 172
    TikTok — 172
    Light Therapy Lamps — 173
    Food — 173
    Aromatherapy and Essential Oils — 174
    Fidget Toys — 175
    Weighted Blankets — 175
    Adult Coloring Book — 176
    Friends — 176
    Mental Health Counselor — 177
    Erin's Story — 177

Conclusion 181
References 185

INTRODUCTION

> *There is a humongous difference between temporary sadness and dissatisfaction with your life—and the sinking desperation that is depression.*
>
> — ELISE JAMESON

Elise was only 14 years old when she was diagnosed with depression. She was extremely frustrated because she felt no one her age really understood her battle with depression. Every second teen thinks they have a Ph.D. and can diagnose themselves with some kind of mental health disorder, such as depression, anxiety, OCD, or even ADHD. If they couldn't concentrate during the first period because of their daily caffeine buzz, they would claim to have ADHD. If one of their friends liked their rooms to be neat and tidy, they would suddenly have OCD. If they had one bad day, it would just as well turn into a bad life and they would diagnose themselves with depression. This bothered Elise because her peers minimized mental health disorders to the point that they became completely desensitized. Some of her peers even thought that those who have been clinically diagnosed with depression are just overdramatic, blaming their hormones or waving it off as being typical teenager mood swings. They had no idea how difficult her daily battle against depression was. It took Elise a very long time to convince herself that she was important and people cared for her. Another misconception that bothered Elise was the fact that most of her peers assumed that if you come from a seemingly "normal" functioning home, you didn't have any reason to be depressed. Many individuals suffering from depression need medication to help them balance the chemicals in their brains. It is easy to judge if you haven't experienced a mental health disorder for yourself.

Do you feel frustrated like Elise? Be careful not to dismiss your symptoms. If you can relate to the stories in this chapter or if you notice that you show most of the symptoms mentioned, go seek help. It can be very frustrating if your friends and family make light of your symptoms but don't get discouraged. This is why raising awareness and proper education is so important.

What is normal? Is it normal to constantly feel miserable, overwhelmed, and out of control? Well, it is more common to feel this way than you might realize. Especially if you are a teenager. In 2020, it was reported that 4,1 million teens in the United States between the ages of 12 and 17 have experienced at least one depressive episode (National Institute of Mental Health, 2022). You are not the only one struggling to fight against anxiety and depression. It is "normal" to feel depressed at this age. Aside from all those cringy talks you hear at school or maybe from your parents about your changing body, you are also experiencing some serious social pressures. Trying to cope with school, maintain a flourishing social life, and stay on top of the latest Tik Tok trends can be overwhelming. It is important to note that there is a major difference between feeling depressed and experiencing a full-blown depressive episode. This book will help you distinguish the difference and teach you coping strategies to help you deal with all these negative emotions and uncertainties.

It might seem to you that your peers have it all together. You might be wondering: "Why me? Why can't I just switch all the negative thoughts off and ignore those overpowering feelings? Why can't I cope like everyone else?" You might even feel completely alone and as if no one understands you. The thought of talking to someone, such as a friend, family member, or even a shrink can cause you to feel even more isolated. If they knew your true thoughts and feelings; they might treat you differently. You already feel damaged and don't want to be treated like a fragile little bird with a broken wing. It can be quite frustrating to deal with all these mixed emotions and not be able to figure it out on your own or get it under control. Although you might think there is something wrong with you for not being able to control what is happening to you, I have good news! You are not supposed to be able to control what happens around you. You are not responsible for the actions, thoughts, or feelings of others. You can, however, have a sense of control over your own behavior, thoughts, and emotions. Now, before you put yourself on a guilt trip, just keep in mind that you were not born with a Ph.D. in Psychology. You were not expected to know how to manage your emotions. This is a skill you need to learn. There are a variety of treatments and techniques discussed in this book that will assist you in your healing journey. Yes, it is a journey–it will take time and effort, but in the end, you will be grateful that you pushed through. You are going to fail, but this doesn't make you a failure. As cliché as it might sound, you will find yourself falling many times, but you will learn to pick yourself up again.

Anxiety and depression are real mental health disorders that can leave you feeling hopeless, helpless, and heartbroken. They have detrimental emotional, physical, and mental side effects. This book will help you understand yourself better and deal with these side effects. It will equip you with the tools necessary to deal with anxiety and depression and find the help you so desperately need.

I decided to write this book because I have worked with teenagers and noticed a significant rise in clinically diagnosed anxiety and depression among 12-to 17-year-olds. For me, this is a great cause for concern. On top of recovering from a terrifying global pandemic, teenagers experience a lot more pressure today than in the past. It just seems unfair that they must deal with all these burdens on their own. As a fellow fighter and huge advocate for mental health awareness, I decided to write this book in the hopes of giving teenagers a fighting chance. It is time to take back control of your life. It is possible to overcome negative thoughts and live a fulfilling life. You can start today. Let's get the ball rolling!

WHAT DOES ANXIETY LOOK LIKE?

> *Even daily stress can turn into worse and more challenging obstacles because, unlike algebraic expressions, students are not taught skills to balance their responsibilities.*
>
> — KAMRIN BAKER

Anxious teens are often misunderstood by their parents and other adults. It is usually made out to be "only a phase." Sometimes those raging hormones are blamed for any kind of negative emotion experienced during adolescence. Yes, it might just be a phase for some, and hormones have a way of messing with your brain's chemistry. However, more often anxiety is a serious mental health disorder that needs some kind of intervention. In this chapter, we will have a look at how common anxiety actually is, what it looks like, and what factors can contribute to feelings of anxiety.

ANXIETY: FIRST THINGS FIRST

Anxiety can leave you feeling alone and isolated. Those who suffer from anxiety tend to have the misconception that no one understands them. Although no one will truly understand the inner battle you have to fight every day, there are teens out there who can relate. A study found that between 2012 and 2017 anxiety among teens rose from 34,1% to 44% (Dekin, 2021). That's a 9,9% increase in only six years! In 2020 5,6 million kids were identified who suffered from anxiety (Osorio, 2022). These numbers continue to rise, especially after the global pandemic. Just keep in mind that these statistics reflect teens who were screened. In other words, there might be even more adolescents struggling with anxiety out there who were not diagnosed. Maybe you are one of those teens who have never been assessed. So, if you think you are alone in this fight against anxiety, think again. Others can relate and there is help.

Let's take a step back and look at what anxiety is. The American Psychological Association defines anxiety as, "an emotion characterized by feelings of tension, worried thoughts, and physical changes like increased blood pressure" (APA, 2022). Individuals suffering from anxiety tend to avoid triggering situations and experience intrusive thoughts as well as specific physical indicators of anxiety, such as excessive perspiration, increased heart rate, dizziness, and trembling. It is important to remember that anxiety is different from fear. Where fear is experienced over the short term and is usually an appropriate response to potential danger, anxiety is a long-term mental health disorder that may have many causes. Anxiety can also be viewed as the expectation of a future threat.

Everyone experiences anxiety. Anxiety is not the enemy. On the contrary, although it might be intense, it is necessary for our survival. Wait, what? Yes, like fear, it is a type of built-in coping mechanism that helps us to keep ourselves safe from potential danger. Anxiety becomes a problem when it starts interfering with our everyday lives. Let's have a look at some common examples. Maybe you can relate.

Lisa has many friends who she likes to hang out with. Although it seems they enjoy spending time with her, a part of her brain tells her that they are only hanging out with her because they feel sorry for her, or they are trying to be nice. She constantly feels as if she is annoying them. Nothing happened that could cause her to feel this way. One day this thought popped up and it hasn't gone away since. Because she feels that she is a nuisance to them, she starts to distance herself from them, causing their friendship to fade. Lisa starts to feel more alone as the days go by.

For Ben, it started more subtly. He always wanted to succeed in school but for some reason, he just couldn't get up in the morning. He wanted to stay in bed all day. His mom would fight with him every morning. Eventually, after a major struggle, he would get dressed and go to school—being late most days. He was always an average learner, usually earning Bs and the occasional A. Slowly, he started losing all interest in school, handing his assignments in late and getting Fs. He avoided going to school even more because he could see the disappointment in his teachers' eyes. Eventually, his parents took him to see a psychiatrist and he was diagnosed with anxiety and depression. The psychiatrist prescribed some medication. Although it brought some relief, his anxiety didn't disappear.

One day, Sam was lying in her bed, about to fall asleep. She had an eventful day—she wrote a test, had a small spat with a friend, had a class presentation, attended debate club, and studied for the test the next day. She was a top-performing student who always earned straight As. While lying in bed that night, she thought she was going to die. Suddenly, without any warning, she experienced chest pains, she started sweating and her heartbeat was out of control. Before she could call for help, she was completely paralyzed. Eventually, these symptoms subsided, and she fell asleep. The next day, she felt anxious at the thought of experiencing these symptoms again. She tried to study for an upcoming exam, but for some reason, she could not focus. As she read a sentence, she would forget what she read. Eventually, she realized that it was pointless to waste time trying to study and she decided to take a nap instead. The next day she was a ball of nerves because she knew that she didn't study enough for the exam. Later that week, the same thing happened when she sat in front of her books, ready to study. Without realizing it, the pressure of achieving top marks, maintaining a social life, and attending all the clubs she was part of, had become too much to bear, and Sam started to experience recurring panic attacks.

You might have noticed that each of these teens' experiences of anxiety is unique. Maybe you can relate, or maybe your experience is completely different. Just because you experience anxiety in a different way than someone else, doesn't mean that you can't find help. There are some common symptoms that can help you identify whether or not you are experiencing chronic anxiety. We will discuss these symptoms in the next section.

RECOGNIZING ANXIETY: COMMON SYMPTOMS

Not one person's experience of anxiety is exactly the same. However, there are some signs and symptoms that can help us identify chronic anxiety. You might notice that you experience three or four of the symptoms listed below. Or, you might even experience all of them.

Wanting Constant Reassurance

Do you constantly find yourself seeking reassurance from your friends, family members, or teachers? You might feel so insecure that you continually need someone to tell you that they like or love you or that you are doing a good job. It is normal to feel uncertain and need reassurance at times. However, when you start doubting yourself constantly and need others' validation, you have anxiety.

Experiencing Specific Symptoms Before Certain Activities or Events

If you find yourself throwing up before a football match, shaking profusely before an exam, or developing a sudden stomach ache before a family event, you may just have found one of your anxiety triggers. We will have a deeper look into these later on in this book.

Avoidance Behavior

It is natural to want to avoid situations that make us feel uncomfortable. If you experience anxiety, you most probably do this regularly. Like Ben, you might want to stay in bed all day to avoid going to school. Or like Lisa, you may isolate yourself because you feel like an intruder. Avoidance behavior can manifest in several ways, including self-sabotaging behavior. For example, not completing that terrifying assignment because you are afraid that you might fail or quitting your passion for dance because you had a few setbacks.

Changes in Sleeping or Eating Patterns

Some people with anxiety stay up for hours at night, overthinking while others seem to stay awake for no apparent reason. Panic attacks and fear of the onset of panic attacks can also keep you up at night. Having nightmares is also a common symptom. The opposite can also be true—to avoid the terrifying world out there, you might find yourself wanting to sleep all the time. Anxiety can also cause you to lose your appetite and excessive amounts of stress can cause indigestion and loss of appetite. On the other hand, anxiety can also result in an increased appetite and cravings. This is due to the production of excessive amounts of cortisol, the stress hormone.

Mood Swings

Anxiety can leave you feeling like you are on an emotional roller coaster and can't get off. Feelings of irritability, nervousness, anger outbursts, sadness, and restlessness are common and can result from those intrusive thoughts and imbalances in your hormone levels. If you have anxiety as a teenager, these mood swings can be exceptionally intense because you are experiencing fluctuations in your hormones and your brain is in the process of undergoing some major developmental changes.

Physical Symptoms

Shaking, racing, or irregular heartbeat, excessive sweating, stomachaches, headaches, fatigue, feeling light-headed or dizzy, hyperventilation or rapid breathing, and digestive issues. You might experience these symptoms all the time or periodically.

Difficulty Concentrating

If you have anxiety, you will probably find it difficult to focus. Tasks that usually seem like a piece of cake suddenly feel like the most daunting and demanding thing on earth. For example, the moment Sam's anxiety spiraled out of control, she simply couldn't focus. Previously, she had no trouble studying, as she was a straight-A student and enjoyed preparing for her tests. She decided to rest instead of study. The next day, she was even more anxious because she didn't study enough, which caused her to become even more anxious.

Can you see that if anxiety is not treated, it can become a vicious cycle? Difficulty concentrating causes a lack of motivation to study that will result in more anxiety right before the test. While writing the exam, Sam will most likely struggle to focus because of the increased anxiety of receiving bad marks. Failure to maintain her excellent standard will make Sam feel even more anxious, causing her to lose even more focus. This cycle will continue until Sam develops coping strategies to deal with her anxiety.

Substance Abuse

Avoidance behavior includes substance abuse. Smoking some weed, having a few stiff drinks, or using some kind of recreational drugs are common for those who have anxiety. Why? Because it brings some temporary relief and tricks you into thinking that you need these substances to cope. These substances momentarily shut off the part of the brain associated with fear. Unfortunately, substance abuse comes with a new set of problems along with, believe it or not, even more anxiety! Because you believe you need these substances to get through the day, you become dependent on them and will do almost anything to feed your habit. Meanwhile, your social life, grades, and personal life are suffering.

Refusing to Go to School

Many teenagers simply refuse to go to school. You might find yourself making up all kinds of excuses not to go to school. It might be that you are afraid of that bully who will humiliate you in front of the entire school, or you are scared that a teacher will pick on you or call you out in front of everyone, or you might be afraid that you will have a panic attack at school.

Anxiety can affect you emotionally, physically, and mentally. Remember that everyone's experience is unique—there is no "one-size-fits-all" indication of how anxiety will manifest. If you can relate to more than half of the symptoms mentioned in the above list, it might be a good idea to get checked out. You can make an appointment with your school counselor or a therapist. Once you have been clinically diagnosed, you can receive the help you need.

WHY IS IT HAPPENING, AND HOW DO I GET IT TO STOP?

No one is anxious without reason. In this section, we will discuss the possible causes of anxiety. Once you have identified the root(s), you can start chopping down that tree and pull out those roots that keep on sprouting.

Genetics

Interestingly, most anxiety disorders start during our teenage years because during this time, new genes emerge and the brain undergoes massive developmental changes. Some people are more prone to develop an anxiety disorder if there is a family history of mental health disorder. If you dig a little deeper into your family tree, you might discover that your mom, aunt, or even great-grandmother struggled with anxiety. It is important to note that although you have a family history of anxiety, other factors also play a role in anxiety disorders. Your genetic predisposition might make you more vulnerable to experiencing anxiety, but certain triggers might aggravate anxiety symptoms. The point is, although you might become anxious easily due to your genes, it is not completely out of your control. You can learn skills to help you cope. You are not doomed to an anxious fate—you can take back control of your life.

On-Going Global Conflicts

Aside from an already uncertain future, teenagers must deal with the fear of violence, such as mass- and school shootings. These shootings are on the rise and are a great cause of concern for both parents and children. In the past, teenagers were not as aware of the ongoing violence out there, but now, they are exposed to this terrifying reality around every corner. Being permanently connected to social media can cause you to feel as if there is no escape or to fear for your own life or the lives of loved ones. It is natural to be concerned about these events, especially if it is thrown in your face all the time.

Social Media

Social media sometimes has a way of making us feel bad about ourselves. It takes a lot of time and dedication to stay on top of all the trends and influencers often use filters and even photoshop to paint a false picture of themselves and their lives. Reels on Instagram and TikTok videos only provide us with snippets of people's lives but we will never truly know what is happening behind the scenes. Although you realize that everything on social media is not real, you still find yourself comparing your outward appearance and even your behavior to these icons. Social media can also cause a significant amount of FOMO ("fear of missing out" for the older folks out there), causing you to check your phone constantly.

Maybe, following influencers is not your thing. Maybe you are one of those influencers. The anxiety of social media will still affect you. The pressure to maintain a perfect image, to constantly post about your life, or check to see how many likes and followers you have, can be taxing.

Let's not forget about the sad reality of cyberbullying. The anonymity of social media makes it a perfect platform to engage in or be a victim of cyberbullying. One study reveals that 59% of teens that are active on the internet have experienced some form of cyberbullying (Sparks,2021).

The Pandemic

Covid-19 turned the whole world upside down. Almost every country went into lockdown, causing anxiety rates to rise, especially among teens. In one study, clinically diagnosed anxiety among teenagers rose from 12,9% pre-pandemic to 20,5% post-pandemic (Guzman, 2023). Although many of us fear becoming sick, it is the unpredictability and uncertainty that causes most of us to become anxious. The future seems uncertain and out of control. The loss of a loved one, an upside-down schooling system, and economic stress all contribute to anxiety.

Trauma

Another major cause of anxiety among teenagers is trauma. What exactly is trauma? According to the American Psychiatric Association, trauma can be "exposure to actual or threatened death, serious injury, or sexual violence" (Harness & Javankbakht, 2021). You don't have to be a direct victim of a traumatic event to be traumatized, simply witnessing a traumatic incident can be traumatizing. Anxiety disorders, such as post-traumatic stress disorder (PTSD) and generalized anxiety disorder (GAD), can be caused by trauma. It can also cause panic attacks and avoidance behavior.

Although it might feel like anxiety has taken over your entire life, and is out of your control, there is hope. You can take back control but you first need to find what works best for you and then make a conscious decision to commit to getting better. Let's be honest; this is not going to be an easy journey, but it is most definitely possible. You can learn how to manage your anxiety.

JAYDEN'S STORY

Seventeen-year-old Jayden struggled with severe social anxiety. He was always a shy kid but it wasn't until he was in high school that he realized he was different. Socializing seemed to be so easy for his peers. He always wondered how everything seemed so effortless for them. Attending a football match or a party was his worst nightmare. He never had many friends and preferred to spend his spare time alone in his room.

His parents were very concerned because at some point he refused to go to school. At first, they felt sorry for him because they could see he was really struggling. They thought it was only a phase that would pass by quickly. Unfortunately, it didn't. Avoiding school only caused Jayden to withdraw even more and some days he wouldn't even come out of his room to eat. His parents were very concerned and realized that it had become a big problem, especially since his future was at stake. They tried everything to get him to go to school. They knew he wasn't being manipulative, that he genuinely had a major fear of going to school but they didn't know why he acted his way. What could they do? They considered homeschooling but were concerned about what would happen after school. Would he be able to go to college? How will he go to work someday if he can't even leave the house? They realized that he would have to learn how to deal with his anxiety so they sent him to a therapist for an evaluation and therapy.

The therapist diagnosed him with social anxiety disorder. He told the therapist that he felt uncomfortable among his friends and had an intense fear of talking in front of others. As soon as a teacher would call his name, he started shaking, his hands became sweaty and his heart would race and, in that moment, he would feel trapped and paralyzed. Jayden was so worried that he would say something dumb or embarrass himself. He would make plans with friends only to cancel them so that after a while, his friends stopped making plans with him because he withdrew completely. He became totally isolated. Fortunately, his therapist taught him some social skills, which helped him to start socializing again. He learned to recognize his triggers and learned how to monitor, challenge and replace his negative thoughts. It took quite a while before Jayden got back on his feet again. It was a difficult road but Jayden eventually learned how to cope with his anxiety.

2

TYPES OF ANXIETY DISORDERS AND INDICATORS

Anxiety comes in many shapes and sizes. It is important to get the necessary treatment and learn coping strategies to help you deal with your anxiety. It is not just "a phase" in your teenage years but a serious mental health condition that will, if not treated, spill over into your adult years. According to the Anxiety and Depression Association of America, an estimated 40 million adults in the United States experience symptoms of anxiety every year, while 28,8% of these adults experience clinically significant symptoms (McLean Hospital, 2022). That is almost one in every three adults.

In this chapter, we will take those first steps in dealing with anxiety by discussing the definition and different types of anxiety disorders. We will also look at some tell-tale physical, emotional, behavioral, and mental signs of anxiety disorders.

WHAT IS AN ANXIETY DISORDER?

Before defining anxiety disorders, it is important to have a clear understanding of what anxiety entails. Anxiety is described as an anticipation of a future concern and is characterized by avoidance behavior and muscle tension. All of us experience anxiety once in a while. However, as soon as anxiety starts interfering with your everyday life, you might be suffering from an anxiety disorder. Anxiety disorders are typically associated with excessive amounts of fear, worry, and nervousness that interfere with school, your social life, everyday tasks, and your overall ability to function. It causes changes in your eating and sleeping habits and negatively affects your mood.

You are generally advised to seek professional help if you suspect that you might have a mental health disorder. Trained professionals have a variety of tools they can use to diagnose psychological disorders. Some of the most well-known tests used to diagnose anxiety disorders include (Lindberg, 2021):

- Hamilton Anxiety Scale
- Social Phobia Inventory

- Zung Self-Rating Anxiety Scale
- Penn State Worry Questionnaire
- Beck Anxiety Scale
- Yale-Brown Obsessive Compulsive Scale
- Generalized Anxiety Disorder Scale

These tests are designed to diagnose anxiety disorders as well as how severe they are. Some tests are designed to diagnose general levels of anxiety, whereas others are used to identify specific anxiety disorders. For example, the Penn State Worry Questionnaire consists of 16 questions, each accompanied by a scale ranging from one, labeled "not at all typical of me," to five, labeled "very typical of me" (NovoPsych, 2021). This test compares your level of worry to that of the normal population and can indicate whether you have social anxiety disorder and/or generalized anxiety disorder. The Social Phobia Inventory is designed to specifically diagnose social anxiety disorders, it consists of 17 questions with a rating scale similar to that of the Penn State Worry Questionnaire (NovoPsych, 2021).

A NOTE ABOUT SELF-DIAGNOSING

Knowing the signs of anxiety disorders can be useful because it can help you realize that you are not just "different" or "weird", but that you might have an anxiety disorder and need help. As they say: Knowledge is power! However, it is still important to allow a trained therapist to make a diagnosis. Self-diagnosing comes with certain risks that can be avoided when you go to a trained professional for help instead.

Almost everyone uses the internet to determine whether or not that cold might be a little more than a cold. Or what home remedies you can use for that rash on your foot. Although some of those home remedies might have worked for you in the past, the reality is that most of what you read on the internet is not medically correct. The same is true for information about mental health issues. When you attempt to self-diagnose using sources from the internet, there is a great chance that you might either misdiagnose or even over-diagnose yourself.

While some mental health disorders are straightforward, others are extremely complicated and difficult to diagnose. There are more than 200 documented mental health disorders, which makes misdiagnosing yourself quite possible. Many psychological disorders share the same traits. For example, attention deficit hyperactivity disorder or ADHD is characterized by inattention and sleep problems, but so are anxiety and depression. Many of these symptoms overlap which makes it hard to make a correct diagnosis. This can cause you to feel even more misunderstood because all those so-called treatments for anxiety on the internet will not help you cope.

Self-diagnosis can also lead to ineffective and even harmful treatment. A therapist can assist you in making the correct diagnosis as well as help you understand your symptoms and treat them accordingly. They can help you paint a picture of how your diagnosis impacts your life and how to deal with the side effects. Some mental health issues can be treated with both psychological and medical interventions. For example, some people need both counseling and prescription medication to help balance the hormones that might contribute to their anxiety. These medications need to be monitored carefully as they can be harmful if not administered properly.

It is also possible to have more than one mental health disorder. If you self-diagnose, you might diagnose yourself with anxiety, but miss the fact that you might also suffer from depression or some kind of personality disorder. Anxiety and depression have very similar symptoms and can easily be confused if not diagnosed by a professional. Some medical conditions can imitate mental health disorders. For example, hyperthyroidism can, just like anxiety, causes heart palpitations, sweaty hands, irritability, and chest pains.

Don't get me wrong, there are many benefits of using the internet and self-diagnosing. It can help you narrow down some of your symptoms and indicate what you might be dealing with. Social media platforms, such as TikTok, normalize mental health issues and can be very informative. Maybe a relatable TikTok video made you realize that you might have anxiety, or it may have even led you to read this book! Many doctors and therapists use TikTok as a platform to inform and help teenagers deal with the ups and downs of adolescence, including coping with anxiety and depression. But be careful who you turn to for advice on social media because some people aren't as educated as they claim to be. Self-diagnostic tools and the internet creates awareness of mental health issues, which helps those who might struggle with anxiety or depression realize that they are not alone. It is just important to remember to seek professional help if you suspect that you suffer from a mental health issue.

TYPES OF ANXIETY DISORDERS

As you might have noticed by now, anxiety is so much more than simply worrying all the time. Anxiety manifests in different ways and in this section, we will dive a little deeper into six of the most common types of anxiety disorders.

Generalized Anxiety Disorder (GAD)

If you find yourself constantly overthinking, thinking of the worst thing that could happen, and obsessing about how you will deal with future dilemmas, you might experience some symptoms of GAD. GAD also comes along with other symptoms, such as fatigue and feeling restless. Worrying all the time is not only time-consuming but also exhausting!

This is probably the most common type of anxiety disorder. Physical symptoms include headaches, stomach aches, and other unexplainable aches and pains GAD is also characterized by the inability to control your worries. It changes over time—some days you might not even notice that you have anxiety, while other days you may feel completely overwhelmed. The source of your worry can also change. For example, one day you might be afraid that you will get sick, and the next day you might stress about putting on too much weight. Maybe you have sleepless nights, worrying if your friends are mad at you, even though you didn't do anything wrong. Or maybe you wonder how you will pass the year before the school year even started! The point is, if you find yourself worrying all the time about what seems to come naturally to others or have sleepless nights, it is worth consulting a professional to determine if you might have GAD.

Social Anxiety Disorder (SAD)

Most of us feel butterflies or are nervous when it is time to give a speech in front of the class, but people with this disorder are terrified when they are required to speak in front of others. Their heart starts to race, their palms sweat profusely, they start shaking, and might even throw up. When invited to large social gatherings, they would rather make up an excuse because the thought of a big group of people is absolutely horrifying.

SAD is also known as social phobia. As you might know, a phobia is an extreme fear of something. Individuals with SAD have an extreme fear of being humiliated, embarrassed, judged, or criticized. In an attempt to avoid being put on the spot, they tend to avoid most, if not all social situations. What seems effortless to others may seem intimidating to them.

Common examples include talking to others, meeting new people, using a public restroom, talking to a cashier, the thought of others seeing how you eat or drink, being called out in class, and speaking in front of others.

Obsessive-Compulsive Disorder (OCD)

You might have heard this term many times before. People tend to claim they have OCD if they like straight lines and equal numbers or if they just enjoy being neat and clean. OCD is much more serious than having your cupboard color-coded and your books arranged alphabetically. It interferes with your daily tasks and can take over your whole life.

People with OCD have thoughts that seem impossible to control. They repeat certain actions over and over again in an attempt to alleviate the anxiety that comes with these thoughts. These actions bring temporary relief but are unfortunately short-lived.

Repetitive hand washing, constantly checking to see if the doors are locked, repetitive counting, constantly rearranging your cupboard and excessive hoarding are all common OCD behaviors. Keep in mind that all of us do some of these actions once in a while. After the announcement of the global pandemic, the whole world started washing their hands repetitively. If you live in an unsafe neighborhood, it is natural to check if the doors are locked for a second or sometimes a third time. However, when those intrusive thoughts become too much to handle and the accompanying actions start to take over your life, you might be suffering from OCD.

Let's have a look at an example. Since Alex was very young, he experienced intrusive thoughts about death and hurting others. Somehow, he knew they were wrong and he tried everything to get the thoughts out of his head but they eventually turned into irrational fears. He would have strange thoughts that didn't make any sense but somehow, he would feel better as soon as he carried out certain actions. Such as, "If you count to 100 and back, your brother won't die," or "If you wash your hands three times, your house won't burn down." He became so obsessed with satisfying that voice in his head that he forgot to hand in assignments and washed his hands until they bled. Somehow it made sense even when it didn't. Alex thought everyone experienced these thoughts until he told his brother about them one day and he finally realized that he needed help.

Panic Disorder

It is all in the name—if you have panic disorder, you have persistent and unexpected panic attacks. Most people who experience panic attacks for the first time might think that they are having a heart attack. This is because panic attacks are very intense and come with a whole list of physical symptoms, such as shaking, dizziness, chest pain, shortness of breath, sweating, racing heart, hot flashes or chills, dry mouth, numbness or pins and needles, and feeling disconnected from your body. These attacks typically last between five and twenty minutes, but if you have experienced them you will know; it can feel like they last a lifetime.

Most individuals with panic disorder have an intense fear of the onset of the next panic attack causing them to avoid certain situations, places, and people that might trigger an attack. If you experience panic attacks, it is important to visit a doctor because it might be a sign of another physical condition. For example, low blood pressure is typically accompanied by a racing heartbeat.

Separation Anxiety Disorder

Separation anxiety naturally occurs in babies, toddlers, and young children. When they experience separation anxiety, they are afraid of being away from their loved ones, such as a parent or caregiver. Older children, teenagers, and adults can also experience separation anxiety but in a different way. They are mostly afraid of something bad happening to their loved ones. Symptoms include an extreme fear of being alone, excessive fear of being away from a specific person, fearing the anticipation of separation, experiencing nightmares about being separated from that specific person, and constant worrying that something might happen to them.

As an example, let's look at Gina's story. She had an unbreakable bond with her grandmother, who not too long ago, was diagnosed with cancer and quickly passed away, leaving Gina heartbroken. How will she ever recover from this tragic loss? Now, she is afraid she might lose her mother as well. She watches her like a hawk and doesn't let her out of her sight. This fear of losing her mother has become so intense that she started making up excuses to avoid going to school. She constantly gets nightmares of her mother dying or disappearing into thin air.

Post-Traumatic Stress Disorder (PTSD)

Not only veterans experience PTSD. Anyone who has experienced or witnessed a traumatic event can have PTSD. The onset of PTSD is usually three months after experiencing or witnessing a traumatic event. However, it can poke out its head many months or even years later. The main features of PTSD include vivid flashbacks, nightmares, reliving the traumatic event in one's mind, feeling numb and depressed, insomnia, being startled easily, irritability, avoiding situations, places, or people associated with the traumatic event, and difficulty concentrating.

Let's look at an example of PTSD. Brittany was only 16 years old when the school shooting occurred. She was a spontaneous, intelligent girl with many dreams. On that sunny day, she wore her favorite pink dress and purple shoes. She was on her way to her English class when she heard a loud "bang" coming from down the hall. There was a moment of silence before the loud noise continued to fill the hallway, students started screaming and teachers were risking their own lives to hide their beloved students. Kids fell to the floor to dodge the flying bullets. Brittany froze, luckily someone grabbed her and hid her under a table. This event changed Brittany's life. She stopped wearing that pink dress, in fact, she stopped wearing anything pink and started having nightmares about people all around her dying. She jumped at the most insignificant noise and her grades dropped significantly. Brittany also had trouble sleeping and started to withdraw from her friends, becoming completely isolated. Her dad noticed this dramatic change in her behavior and took her to see a counselor who diagnosed her with PTSD.

INDICATORS OF ANXIETY DISORDERS

Physical Indicators

Anxiety can manifest in a variety of ways. When you experience a potential threat, your body naturally wants to protect itself. You might have already heard of the fight-or-flight response. When you notice a threat, your body automatically produces stress hormones—cortisol and adrenaline. These hormones prepare your body to either flee or fight back by supplying more energy, blood, and oxygen to your muscles. This is why your heart starts pounding, you breathe faster and sometimes you can feel your muscles tense up. In the past, when people faced physical threats such as lions and bears, their bodies would go into "survival mode" by activating the fight-or-flight response and when these threats passed, their bodies would return to normal. However, the threats we experience today don't necessarily come and go as they did in the past. We live in uncertain times causing us to feel a lot of pressure to perform. Our bodies are aware of this and stay stuck in this "survival mode." This is why those who have anxiety experience so many physical symptoms that seem to have no medical cause.

Physical indicators include:

- Feeling tired or weak
- Insomnia
- Headaches
- Increased heart rate
- Sweating
- Muscle tension or pain
- Shortness of breath
- Constantly feeling sick

Focusing on these physical symptoms can cause even more anxiety. It is easy to grab a bottle of pills to ease your throbbing headache, but unfortunately, pills might cause a bigger problem and won't fix the root problem of these symptoms. If you put a band-aid on a wound without properly cleaning it, it might cause an infection. There are simple strategies you can use to relieve some of these physical symptoms.

1. Practice consciousness—if you feel that your heartbeat is increasing, your muscles start tensing up or that headache is coming on, stop for a second and breathe. Take a second to think about what is happening. Did something trigger these symptoms? What emotions are you experiencing?

2. Distract yourself—by distracting yourself, you can take your mind off of your symptoms. The chances are that your symptoms will go away in the process. You can divert your attention by going for a walk, cuddling with a pet, getting yourself a snack or something to drink, doing some chores, taking a bath, or reading a book. You can also try some relaxation techniques, such as deep breathing. There are many apps available that will help you find your calm. Try to figure out what activities will help you to relax.
3. Reassure yourself—remember that although the physical symptoms you are experiencing are intense, they are not harmful. If you feel uncertain, visit a doctor to do a screening to ensure there is no underlying cause of your symptoms. Keep in mind that your physical symptoms should go away as soon as the anxiety is reduced.

Mental Indicators

Anxiety has a nasty way of messing with your mind. It might seem as if you have no control over your thoughts. The most common mental indicators of anxiety include:

- Racing thoughts—these thoughts usually come out of nowhere. They are usually quick and can cause you to worry about one thing or a few things at the same time. For example, "I have a big test next week, where will I get time to study? What if I fail? I don't want to disappoint my parents. I wonder if my friends still like me. I don't deserve to have them as my friends."
- A feeling of impending doom—anxiety has a way of letting you feel as if something bad is about to happen all the time. This feeling can be quite terrifying.
- Overthinking—this usually causes you to obsess about something, wondering if you did the right thing and thinking of solutions to a problem that doesn't exist. It is common to overthink at night when you are all alone and everything around you is quiet. For example, "I hope I didn't offend my friend by telling her I need to study rather than hang out with her. What if she finds someone else to hang out with? What if she hates me now? I have to make it up to her, but how? Maybe we can hang out this weekend, or we can study together. But I won't be able to concentrate. Maybe I should just hang out with her and study tonight." Does

this sound familiar? Overthinking can be exhausting!

- Difficulty concentrating—struggling to focus is one of the most common mental indicators of anxiety disorders. Before the anxiety started, you might have had no difficulties studying for a test. Now, you might find it so difficult to study or focus in class that your grades have dropped. Don't worry, it is completely normal if you struggle with anxiety. Once you learn some coping strategies, you will notice that your concentration has improved.
- Dissociation—dissociation occurs when you disconnect from what is happening around you. To others, it might seem as if you are daydreaming or thinking about something important when you might not be thinking of anything at all. Dissociation causes you to feel emotionally numb and detached. You temporarily lose touch with reality.
- Always feeling on edge—you constantly feel tense and jumpy. Slightly loud or sudden noises startle you. You feel restless and can't sit back and relax.
- Irritability—if you feel irritable, small things that usually didn't bother you, make you angry, or feel irritated. Suddenly your sister's

breathing gets on your nerves or the label on your shirt which has been there for two years now, irritates you like never before.

Sometimes you don't have the time or resources to fully examine, detangle and deal with your uncontrollable thoughts. During these times, you need quick hacks that will pull you through your day. Check out the list below for some tips for dealing with these mental symptoms:

1. Trick your brain with deep breathing—first, you close your eyes and take a deep breath. Hold your breath for a few seconds. Then, release it, making sure you blow all the air out of your lungs by engaging your abdominal muscles. Diaphragmatic or deep breathing is an effective way of calming your body and mind because it sends a signal to your brain that there is no immediate threat or danger. Different parts of your brain respond by triggering the rest-and-digest response (the opposite of the flight-or-fight response). Your body and mind will then begin to calm down.
2. Journaling for the win—one of the best and scientifically proven strategies to deal with anxiety is journaling. Write the date, place, and

any other details down about your current situation. This will help you identify patterns and monitor your progress. Now write down all those intrusive thoughts and read through them carefully. Are they valid or irrational? Determine the level of anxiety. You can use a scale from one to ten. Write down any other feelings you might be experiencing.

3. Use music as therapy—music can be an excellent way to distract yourself from those disturbing thoughts. You can either make music or listen to music. If you know how to play an instrument, take a moment to practice a song. Studies have shown that playing a musical instrument releases emotional tension and reduces anxiety (DeMarco, 2022). You can also listen to some of your favorite music. Start by making a playlist with your favorite songs. Try to add songs that you can associate with happy memories or that make you feel relaxed. Whenever you feel tense, close your eyes and listen to your playlist.

4. Grounding exercises—this is an effective therapeutic tool that you can use to connect yourself to the present moment by using your senses. An easy one you can practice anywhere is the 5-4-3-2-1 technique. First, you name five

things you see. Then, identify four things you can hear. Next, you find three things with different textures that you can touch. Now, you try to find two things that you can smell. Lastly, find something you can taste, such as a small snack or a beverage. While doing this exercise, make sure that you are present and in the moment. Take in every detail you possibly can to avoid going back to that dark place. If you notice that your thoughts start wandering again, refocus by directing your attention to what you can see, hear, feel, smell, and taste.

5. Try the art of distraction—a healthy distraction can be very effective to get your mind off of those racing thoughts. We can't control everything around us. One of the best ways to let go of this tendency to control the uncontrollable is by distracting yourself. Remember, hours of scrolling through social media, using drugs or alcohol and overeating aren't healthy ways to distract yourself. Healthy ways to distract yourself include learning something new, going for a walk, watching a funny show, re-watching your favorite series, reading a book, or learning a new dance routine.

Emotional Indicators

Believe it or not, all emotions are important—even the bad ones. Although we don't always understand them, they are there for a reason; to tell us something we need to know about our minds and bodies. Anxiety itself is an emotional disorder and comes with a whole list of uncomfortable emotions. Studies show that people with GAD have lower levels of emotional sensitivity (Rutter et al., 2019). In other words, if you have GAD you would most likely find it difficult to recognize emotions, such as sadness, anger, and happiness. Emotions are very complex and abstract, even for the "average" individual. Now, just imagine how difficult it must be to understand all those mixed feelings when you have GAD. To avoid or suppress these confusing emotions people with anxiety sometimes resort to unhealthy coping strategies, such as self-harming, alcohol and substance abuse, and overeating. In some cases, individuals develop additional mental disorders, such as eating disorders and depression.

It is important to remember that anxiety is rooted in stress. Stress is important for our survival, but once it starts lingering and becomes overwhelming, it can change your brain's chemistry, influencing your emotions. Emotions linked to anxiety include:

- anger
- sadness
- irritation
- isolation
- nervousness
- restlessness

The following hacks can help you to manage these emotional indicators:

1. Move your body—low-impact exercises are especially effective in helping you manage negative emotions, such as yoga and tai chi. They help you to slow down, refocus your attention, and breathe deeply. You can either attend a class at your nearest gym or, if you feel more comfortable, you can search for these exercises on YouTube or download an app.
2. Challenge those intrusive thoughts—once you find yourself feeling anxious about something, identify the thoughts associated with the feeling and give yourself a pep talk. Let me explain by using an example. Your friend says she wants to talk to you after school. Immediately your brain starts racing. "What have I done wrong? She must be mad about something. Maybe she hates me or doesn't want to be friends anymore."

Once these thoughts start running around in your head, stop and take a deep breath. Give yourself a quick pep talk: "Maybe she just wants to talk. She might have a question about our chemistry project. Maybe she wants to hang out later this week." Remember that you are not a fortune-teller or a mind-reader, so take those thoughts and turn them into something positive before you start ruminating on something that would most likely not happen.

3. Use Progressive Muscle Relaxation (PMR)—this relaxation technique helps you to counteract the flight-or-fight response by slowly calming the body down. Before you start, make sure that you are comfortable. You can either lie down or sit in a comfortable chair. Take slow, deep breaths. Repeat this about five times. Now, starting with your feet, tighten the muscles in your toes. Hold it for a few breaths before releasing slowly. Repeat this exercise with every muscle group until you reach your shoulders, neck, and face. Repeat this exercise if you notice that a specific part of your body is very stiff. When you are done, take a few more deep breaths and feel how relaxed your body is.

Behavioral Indicators

Have you ever wondered why you do certain things? Don't be hard on yourself; anxiety has a way of making us do some bizarre things. Every behavioral response has a cause. Let's look at a few examples:

- Isolating behavior—in your mind, it makes sense to isolate yourself from others and not enjoy life because you want to deal with your anxiety on your own. You don't want to burden others with your problems and believe that no one else will truly understand what you are going through. Anxiety is exhausting, so you are tired all the time and want to recuperate on your own. Although this makes sense in your head, this self-sabotaging behavior only worsens your anxiety symptoms. Having more time to yourself to ruminate and overthink causes you to withdraw even more and increases your anxiety.
- Agoraphobia—also known as a fear of leaving the house. Many are afraid of leaving the house because of something bad that might happen. Often agoraphobia is caused by the fear of the onset of a panic attack. Panic attacks are not only terrifying but can leave you feeling

embarrassed and helpless, especially if there are many witnesses.

- Compulsions—these are very common in those who have OCD. They use certain repetitive actions in an attempt to ease or get rid of negative thoughts. Some compulsions make sense while others don't. For example, the fear of germs can cause you to repetitively wash your hands. This makes some sense. Other behaviors might not make any sense at all, such as avoiding cracks on the ground because you believe if you step on one, you will fail your test.
- Nervous tics—many people develop tics when they feel nervous. This can include excessive blinking, rubbing your hands, biting your nails, winking, shaking your leg up and down, or clearing your throat.
- Problems at school—many children and teenagers who have anxiety get into trouble all the time. This is because anxiety causes emotional dysregulation. In other words, they don't understand all these overwhelming feelings so they act out. They constantly feel restless and can't concentrate so some of them will disrupt the class while others withdraw

completely even though they want to participate.

Some additional anxiety hacks include:

1. Clench your fists—this is an easy exercise you can do anywhere. As soon as you feel your body tensing up, or you are withdrawing into your world again, place your hands on your legs or let them hang, take deep breaths, and clench your fists as hard as you can. Continue to breathe slowly while releasing your fists. Stretch your fingers as far as possible and repeat this exercise if necessary.
2. Repeat a calming mantra—while breathing deeply, repeat a calming phrase, such as "I am safe," "I am enough," or, "this too shall pass."
3. Look at your surroundings—when you feel overwhelmed, distract yourself by noticing your surroundings. You can look at all the different colors around you, count the books on a shelf or feel the texture of whatever is nearest to you. This is an effective grounding exercise that refocuses your attention on the here and now.

Remember that the best hack to combat anxiety is awareness and education. Get to know yourself, how your symptoms manifest, and which techniques work best for you. If you know what is happening to you and why it is happening, you will be able to use some of the simple techniques discussed in this chapter to relieve your anxiety and keep yourself grounded. Keep in mind that these strategies are quick fixes that will help you recuperate yourself in the moment and can be especially helpful to manage panic attacks and anxiety attacks. We will have a look at some other techniques later in this book that will help you cope with anxiety in the long run. But first, it is important to know the difference between anxiety attacks and panic attacks.

3

PANIC ATTACKS VS. ANXIETY ATTACKS–DIFFERENCES AND COPING STRATEGIES

> *If it's beginning to interfere with your life, if you're more fearful, or if you're avoiding doing things that provoke the symptoms, that's when you need to seek help.*
>
> — CHERYL CARMIN

The first panic attack Chris experienced was terrifying. He was in the middle of a big football game, when suddenly he felt his chest tightening, turning into a sharp pain. Everything around him became distant, his heart raced and his breathing became uncontrollably fast. The first thought he had was that something was seriously wrong—he was having a heart attack! He collapsed on the field in front of a whole crowd of spectators. The medical response team immediately carried him off the field on a stretcher. After a thorough medical examination by the doctor, it turned out that Chris didn't have a heart attack after all. Nothing was medically wrong with him. Confused, he asked the doctor what could have happened out there. The doctor claimed that he had a panic attack. Chris was baffled. But how could this have happened so suddenly? And in front of all those people! His parents sent him to a counselor and it turned out that Chris had been struggling with anxiety for a while. All the pressure to perform in school, do well in football to get a college scholarship, and maintain his social life became too much for him to handle.

Have you ever experienced a sudden panic attack like Chris? Maybe you were always aware of your anxiety and have experienced an anxiety attack. Whatever the case might be, keep on reading.

PANIC VS. ANXIETY

This section will describe panic attacks and anxiety attacks: What they look like, what they feel like, and what could set them off. Although there are differences between panic attacks and anxiety attacks, they should be addressed immediately because both are serious.

Panic Attacks

Panic attacks are not as rare as you might think. An estimated 14% of adults experience panic attacks every year (Guzman, 2023b). These panic attacks are experienced mostly by adults in their 30s and are more prevalent in women than men. So, what is a panic attack? A panic attack can be described as a sudden feeling of intense anxiety or fear and is accompanied by physical symptoms, such as shortness of breath, sweating, racing heart, and dizziness. Some experts believe that panic attacks act like false alarms (National Institute of Mental Health, 2022). According to them, the body's survival mode is overactive, causing it to suddenly trigger the flight-or-fight response without any potential threat. Panic attacks can be physically immobilizing. The onset of a panic attack can either be expected or unexpected and typically last ten minutes. The triggers or causes of panic attacks are usually unclear. However, if you frequently experience panic attacks, a mental health professional can help you to determine possible triggers and how to deal with them. Certain medical conditions can cause panic attacks, such as hyperthyroidism (an overactive thyroid gland), withdrawal from certain medications, some stimulants, such as caffeine or cocaine, high blood pressure, and mitral valve prolapse (a heart condition). Therefore, if you experience panic attacks, be sure to visit a doctor for a thorough medical screening.

Symptoms of a panic attack include:

- lightheadedness
- rapid or irregular heartbeat
- nausea
- hot flashes or chills
- shaking
- numbness
- chest pain
- stomach pain
- sweating
- difficulty breathing

If you experience frequent panic attacks, you might have panic disorder, which means you also constantly worry about when the next panic attack might happen. These panic attacks usually occur out of nowhere, leaving you feeling helpless. You try to avoid places or situations that might trigger panic attacks. Some people with panic disorder develop agoraphobia because they are afraid that they might experience a panic attack when they leave the safety of their homes.

Anxiety Attacks

The Diagnostic and Statistical Manual of Mental Disorders (DSM) doesn't provide us with a clear description of what an anxiety attack entails. Defining an anxiety attack is subjective because it can be used to describe a variety of anxiety indicators. Anxiety attacks are usually caused by anticipating a potential threat. For example, say you are walking down a dark alley and start to worry about how safe it is. Your mind starts to race and you are afraid that someone might jump out with a knife or gun and hurt you. Gradually, your heartbeat increases, your breathing becomes faster, and you feel nervous and agitated. You are experiencing an anxiety attack.

On the other hand, say you are walking down the street, minding your own business, not worrying about anything, and suddenly someone jumps out from behind a bush and points a gun at you. Your body immediately responds to the threat; you start sweating, your heart beats faster, your breathing increases and your chest begins to ache. You are experiencing a panic attack. It is easy to confuse an anxiety attack with a panic attack because they share many symptoms. Anxiety attacks are not as intense as panic attacks and develop progressively. They also have specific triggers that are easier to identify. Anxiety attacks typically last longer than panic attacks—they can last for hours or even days. However, an anxiety attack can develop into a panic attack.

The Differences

Before we discuss the differences between panic and anxiety attacks, we are going to do a quick activity. Below are three scenarios. Your job is to identify which scenarios describe panic attacks and which describe anxiety attacks. Let's go!

Scenario 1

One day, you are scrolling through social media. You come across a video that has gone viral in the past 24 hours. This video shows how kids are being quarantined in their schools because there has been a sudden outbreak of a new disease. Police officers are guarding the school and delivery trucks dropping food at the school's entrance with hazmat suits on. You are not sure if this video was recorded during the 2020 pandemic or if it happened recently.

You feel tired and worry about what the future might hold. You have an essay that is due tomorrow but you can't focus. Suddenly this assignment feels overwhelming. Will you be able to finish your essay on time? What will happen if another pandemic hits the world?

Scenario 2

It is midnight already and for some reason you can't fall asleep. It seems like your brain simply can't switch off. You have so many racing thoughts. You keep on thinking of possible catastrophes that might happen. What if...? It feels as if your heart is beating outside your chest. Completely exhausted, you turn around to check the time. It is 3 am already!

Scenario 3

You are hanging out with friends at the mall. You are laughing, making jokes, and having a good time. All of a sudden, you feel your heart rate increasing, you can hear the blood rushing through your body, you feel a sharp pain in your chest and you can't breathe. Are you having a heart attack? Are you going to die? It certainly feels like it! An intense fear washes over you and you want to escape. You excuse yourself and go outside.

Anxiety attack or panic attack?

Answer time!

The first scenario is an example of a normal anxiety response to a potentially threatening situation. It is natural and understandable to feel stressed if there might be another pandemic on the way. An uncertain future, deadlines, and traumatic past experiences, such as the 2020 pandemic can trigger anxiety. Because anxiety attacks are subjective, we can classify this scenario as an anxiety attack.

The second scenario demonstrates an anxiety attack. This scenario is more intense than the first one. If you experience episodes like this during the night, you might find treatment for anxiety very helpful. Although anxiety attacks cause physical symptoms, they are also characterized by intrusive and racing thoughts. They build up slowly as you experience possible threats or triggers.

The third scenario is a perfect example of a panic attack. They usually come out of nowhere, without any cause or provocation. Panic attacks can also be expected, for example as a result of exposure to a certain phobia. They are much more intense than anxiety attacks. Most individuals who experience panic attacks feel as though they are dying. The physical symptoms are more extreme than those of anxiety attacks. Treatment for panic attacks can be very beneficial, as a trained therapist can help you identify and deal with potential triggers.

As you might have noticed in the above scenarios, anxiety attacks can either be mild, moderate, or severe, whereas panic attacks are disruptive and therefore more severe than anxiety attacks. The flight-or-fight response is more intense with panic attacks and comes suddenly. A panic attack can subside just as fast as it appeared. Although anxiety attacks aren't as intense, they tend to last longer than panic attacks.

WHAT TO DO WHEN YOU'RE HAVING AN ATTACK

In this section, we will look at some techniques you can use when you are experiencing an attack. It is important to remember that we are all unique. Some of the strategies might work wonders for you, while others might not work at all. There is no one-size-fits-all approach. Test these techniques and see which works best for you.

You might find it difficult to remember these strategies in the beginning. Remember that you are already overwhelmed. Your thoughts and emotions are all over the place, so don't be hard on yourself. Don't become discouraged or annoyed if you forget something. It will take time and some patience but you will get there.

Eat Some Sour Candy

Licenced trauma therapist, Micheline Maalouf, shared this helpful tip on Tik Tok (Michelson, 2021). Focusing on the physical symptoms or trying to fight against them will only make them worse. This might seem like common sense, but if you are overwhelmed by the incapacitating effects of a panic attack, all you can think about are those physical symptoms and how to make them stop. Grabbing something sour to eat (the more sour the better) as soon as you feel a panic attack coming on, can distract you and relieve some of the physical symptoms, possibly helping you to avoid having a full-blown panic attack. Why does this trick work? Because it shocks your senses and grounds you by diverting your attention to the sour taste and away from the physical symptoms of a panic attack.

Try Some Ice

Sucking on an ice cube or rubbing some ice at the back of your neck has the same effect on your senses as eating something sour. It distracts your mind and body from the panic attack. This trick works well if you are at home, at a friend's house, or in a restaurant. Just grab some ice out of the freezer or take some out of your drink and start sucking.

Read Something Backwards

This technique will not only help you relieve some anxiety but might have you laughing as well. So many things happen in your mind and body at the same time when you are having an anxiety or panic attack. Your brain can't do two complex tasks at the same time, so look for the nearest magazine or book and start reading something backward. This will divert your attention completely and you may even start laughing in the process. Laughter will increase those happy hormones, boost your mood, and relieve even more anxiety.

Channel Your Inner Artist

Words can be difficult to express, even on paper sometimes. Some people prefer to journal while others find it stressful to put their thoughts on paper. If you can't put your worries in words, draw instead. Draw whatever comes to mind. Try to draw something funny, for instance, draw yourself as a cartoon character. Or draw your pet as a cartoon, add speech bubbles, and think of silly things they might say if they could talk. This technique works well when you feel an anxiety attack approaching. Remember, if drawing isn't your thing, try something else. But if you never tried this technique before, give it a go; you might discover a hidden talent.

Breathe

You might be tired of reading about this one, but breathing is very effective in relieving anxiety, especially the physical effects thereof. When you experience a panic attack, your breathing increases dramatically. Sometimes you even lose your breath. The moment you realize that you have trouble breathing, you will probably panic even more, causing you to become even more breathless. As soon as you feel a panic attack coming on, focus on your breathing. Are you breathing correctly? If you find that only your chest and shoulders are moving as you are breathing, you are breathing incorrectly. Instead, take slow, deep breaths in through your nose, making sure that your abdomen is also expanding. Then slowly release your breath through your mouth. Repeat this until you feel your body calming down. Remember, when you are on the brink of having an attack or you are already experiencing an attack, it might be difficult to stop and focus on your breathing. Try your best to be persistent.

Hydrate and Keep Your Blood Sugar in Check

What sometimes feels like the beginning of a panic attack, might not be one at all. Low blood sugar levels and being dehydrated can cause a similar response to a panic attack. When you start feeling dizzy, your breathing increases and your heart starts pounding, grab a snack and take a sip of water. If your blood sugar levels dropped or you were somewhat dehydrated boom! Problem fixed. If it was the start of a panic attack, great. Eating or drinking can also divert your attention, relieving some—or all—of the symptoms of a panic attack. Make sure to keep some water and a small snack at hand for when the panic comes knocking on your door.

Sharing is caring, so don't be afraid to tell close friends and family about your panic attacks. All of us need a support network, whether we struggle with anxiety or not. Share these tips with them so that they can help the next time your anxiety starts flaring up. They can remind you to breathe, give you something sour or dig in the freezer for some ice cubes. You never know, they might find these tips and tricks useful in their own lives one day.

Although these tips can be very helpful in surviving a panic attack, they are only short-term solutions. The best way to deal with panic attacks is to follow a long-term approach. Consistent therapy sessions will assist you in decreasing the frequency of your panic attacks in the long run.

NEAL'S STORY

One day Neal was running on the treadmill at the gym. Suddenly he felt lightheaded and his heart felt like it was beating out of his chest. No, he wasn't out of shape. In fact, he was in the best shape of his life. He felt a pain shoot through his chest and immediately started to worry about his heart.

The next day, he visited the doctor who decided to do an EKG, but his heart was in good shape. The doctor told Neal that he might have experienced a panic attack. Neal realized that he was under a lot of pressure. He recently started a new business venture and was working 16 hours a day. One of his friends was terminally ill and he had also started training with a personal trainer. He was experiencing a great amount of physical, emotional, and financial stress. He realized that many family members had anxiety and that he too experienced anxiety from childhood.

Neal decided to take things into his own hands. He started avoiding places that might seem triggering. He made all kinds of arrangements to go out as little as possible. He mostly ran his business from home, however, this was not always possible. One day, he had a panic attack while driving on the freeway. After two and a half years of this avoidance behavior, Neal realized that his anxiety was not improving. It got even worse. He decided to see a licensed therapist, who diagnosed him and helped him understand agoraphobia and panic disorder. The therapist also taught him how to identify and manage triggers. Finally, he received treatment that actually worked.

Sunny, on the other hand, was diagnosed with anxiety and depression when she was only 13 years old. Only days after being diagnosed, she experienced her first panic attack. After seeing a therapist for two years, she lost her cousin in a car accident and things started to spiral out of control. Her anxiety and depression got worse—she struggled to cope and her grades dropped. She started depending on others to distract her from what was going on and somehow, she believed that her happiness depended on others. She started reading personal stories of others who also struggled with anxiety and realized that she wasn't alone. This was all she needed to put her back on her road to recovery once more.

The death of Sunny's cousin was a major setback. Even though she was seeing a therapist for two years, this event caused her to experience a relapse. Setbacks are normal and even expected. Reading stories like these can help one find advice.

Don't take matters into your own hands as Neal did. You might just make things worse. Remember, seeking treatment from a trained professional is the most effective way to deal with anxiety and panic attacks in the long term.

FIRST-AID KIT

Most of us have first-aid kits in our homes to help us deal with minor injuries, such as cuts or burns. You need special training or certification to clean a wound or treat a first-degree burn.

The tips and tricks in this chapter work like a first aid kit—they provide you with practical quick-fix solutions that will help you when you need them most. Items that you need in your "mental first-aid kit" include:

- sour candy
- an ice pack
- something to read
- a sketchbook and pencil
- a snack and some water

Remember that there is a difference between having an anxiety attack and a panic attack. The onset of an anxiety attack takes time while a panic attack occurs abruptly and mostly out of the blue. The physical symptoms of an anxiety attack are not as intense as those of a panic attack. A panic attack typically lasts up to ten minutes, whereas an anxiety attack can last up to hours and even days. In the next chapter, we will look at another common mental health disorder that teenagers struggle with—depression.

4

WHAT DOES DEPRESSION LOOK LIKE?

Tracy was outgoing and spontaneous and didn't seem depressed. She grew up in a wealthy family, was a talented swimmer, and excelled in academics. Her parents were supportive and she was very popular among her friends. Although she did extremely well with her grades, swimming formed a great part of her identity. After school, she couldn't wait to get into the water and she planned her whole day around her swimming schedule.

Unfortunately, in her sophomore year, it felt like her whole world was falling apart. She was involved in a car accident and sustained some serious injuries. It felt like her life was over because suddenly she couldn't participate in any physically strenuous activities, including swimming. She lost her sense of belonging and started to withdraw. As she isolated herself, she started getting thoughts about hurting herself.

Tracy tried to hide her depression from her friends and family. She still made plans with her friends but would make up excuses and cancel. At night, she would toss and turn; unable to sleep. During the day, she would pray for the day to end because she was not only tired but felt completely hopeless.

Eventually, Tracy started cutting herself. Day in and day out, thoughts of suicide would haunt her. One day, she felt like she was at the end of the line. She had two choices; either she would end it all or she would talk to someone before she decided to do anything drastic. She thought it best to speak to a trusted friend before she did anything she might regret. Fortunately, her friend immediately told her mother, who then realized her daughter was acting differently and might be struggling with depression. Her mother immediately decided to take Tracy to a therapist who would help her get the help she needed.

The Centers for Disease Control and Prevention (CDC) found in a study that 44% of teenagers in the United States experience "persistent feelings of sadness and hopelessness" (Rice, 2022). If you or someone you know are struggling with feelings of hopelessness and sadness, don't hesitate to take that first step—talk to someone. The first step is usually the most difficult. You are not alone. There is hope for a brighter future.

In this chapter, we will have a look at the symptoms of depression and what you can do about it.

DEPRESSION IS...

Depression, like anxiety, is on the rise. Between 2019 and 2022, depression among teenagers rose from 37% to 44% (Rice, 2022). That is 7% in only three years! In the past, teens weren't as aware of the emotional struggles of their peers as they are today. Depression and anxiety have become such a problem that 70 % of teenagers in the United States recognize it as a major problem among their friends (Menasce Horowitz et al., 2019).

The pandemic played a significant role in these increasing rates of anxiety and depression. Not only did the future seem uncertain, but the loss of physical, social, and emotional contact made things worse.

Social connections are extremely important for all human beings, especially for teenagers' mental health. It is our relationships that offer us the support we need to bounce back after going through a difficult experience. Social connections are responsible for a major part of our social and emotional development. It provides us with a sense of belonging and security. As a teenager, you are on a journey to find your own identity. To discover this new identity, you become more independent and naturally place greater value on your relationships with your friends. If you struggle to connect with your peers, feelings of isolation increase, and your mental well-being declines. Many studies show that a lack of quality relationships with peers during adolescence increases the risk of mental health issues, including depression (Rice, 2022).

During the pandemic, we resorted to technology to stay connected to each other. However, the use of technology and social media doesn't provide enough support. On the contrary, studies found that increased social media use can be associated with a rise in mental health issues among teenagers (Winstone et al., 2021). Now, you can only imagine how the lockdown during the pandemic affected teenagers' mental well-being all over the world!

So, what is depression? Depression is more than having the occasional blue Monday or feeling down. Yes, you are most likely experiencing some ups and downs thanks to those raging hormones, but what if you feel down all the time, with no hope for the future? Depression is a serious mental health concern that requires a diagnosis and treatment. It is characterized by persistent feelings of sadness and a loss of interest in activities that are usually enjoyable. It influences your thoughts, emotions, and behavior. So, what does this mean?

Does This Sound Like You?

Let's go back to Tracy's story. She was outgoing and enjoyed spending time with her friends. As soon as the depression set in, she lost all interest in spending time with them. She started getting thoughts about hurting herself and after a while, they turned into suicidal thoughts. She acted on some of those thoughts by cutting herself and became more isolated, felt hopeless, and wanted to give up.

Cindy's experience with depression was a little different than Tracy's. From a very young age, Cindy felt that she was different from everyone else. She never understood how other children could laugh and play without a care in the world. She always had this heavy feeling hovering over her. Her mother suffered from depression and so Cindy taught herself to cook, clean, and take care of other household tasks when she was about ten years old. Her father worked hard to provide for the family and would come home late to eat and sleep, only to be up early again the next day to go to work.

When she hit her teenage years, this heavy feeling turned into sadness and worthlessness. She felt like there was no reason for her existence except to care for her mentally ill mother. She knew her mother loved her, but she simply couldn't show it. She had no friends and wasn't exceptionally talented. No matter what she did, she couldn't concentrate and started failing one subject after the other. She found comfort in food and became somewhat overweight, causing her to feel even more worthless.

Cindy was tired all the time even though she slept a lot. After school, she would come home, take a nap, wake up and make dinner, do some homework, or fall asleep trying. Every morning she would drag herself out of bed. Her feet always felt heavy so she walked extremely slowly.

Unlike Tracy, Cindy might have had depression since she was very young. Tracy's depression started soon after the car accident, whereas Cindy always felt burdened. Tracy's behavior changed quickly compared to Cindy's behavior who changed gradually over time. Maybe you can relate to one of these stories or maybe your experience is completely different. Whatever the case may be, depression manifests in different shapes and sizes. The important thing is to speak up and seek help.

In the next section, we will have a look at some signs and symptoms of depression.

DEPRESSION: WHAT TO EXPECT

To be clinically diagnosed with major depressive disorder, you have to experience persistent feelings of sadness and hopelessness for at least two weeks. Look out for the following signs and symptoms if you suspect that you or a loved one might be struggling with depression:

- constantly feeling sad
- feelings of hopelessness
- irritability
- low self-esteem
- feelings of guilt
- loss of interest in previously enjoyable activities
- social withdrawal
- feeling bored all the time
- sleeping problems (either sleeping too much or trouble falling asleep)
- changes in weight and appetite (eating too much or too little)
- aches and pains such as headaches or stomach aches
- thoughts of self-harm

- suicidal thoughts
- decline in school performance
- fatigue
- anxiety
- finding it difficult to make decisions

Feelings of sadness and hopelessness can be disguised in many ways, including irritability. Many teenagers who are depressed sometimes come across as angry. Anger can be expressed in different ways, including through frustration, annoyance at the most trivial provocation, nasty or sarcastic remarks, or anger outbursts. Why do some teenagers express anger when they are actually sad? Well, you see, it is much easier to feel angry than to feel hopeless and anger usually acts like the tip of an iceberg. Close your eyes and imagine an iceberg in the middle of the ocean. You see a small island made of ice. Now, wearing a complete scuba suit, you dive into the ocean. Under the water you see a massive block of ice, maybe a mile deep and two miles wide. What you see on the surface is rage, frustration, and irritability, but what lies underneath is much bigger. Under the water, you can see sadness, despair, hopelessness, uncertainty, rejection, loneliness, and anxiety.

We all feel angry and frustrated sometimes, but if anger is a symptom of depression, it looks a little bit different than being irritated by your parents nagging you to do your chores or to put your phone away while having dinner. If you experience anger as a symptom of depression, you constantly feel annoyed and angry, whether you are at home or school. It is also accompanied by other symptoms mentioned in the list above, specifically fatigue. If you experience high levels of energy, together with anger, you might have anxiety instead. Anxiety and depression can easily be misdiagnosed due to their similarities. This is why it is important to be diagnosed by a trained professional.

To demonstrate how anger can be a symptom of depression, we are going to have a look at Jayden's story. Jayden was a quiet, introverted teen who was an avid gamer. He enjoyed playing games online with his friends, especially until late at night. His parents were fighting most of the time, so he found comfort in connecting with this online community.

One day his parents announced that they were going to get divorced. Although Jayden saw it coming, he was angry for some reason and his behavior started to change. He was tired all the time, he stopped playing games, his grades dropped, he didn't feel like eating or even taking a shower and he felt annoyed all the time. Everything got on his nerves—the sound of the neighbor's lawn mower, his mother's voice, a stranger's smile, and even his beloved dog's wagging tail irritated him. His mother knew he was more reserved than the other kids; but, she noticed that he started to withdraw completely and had sudden anger outbursts about the smallest things. She decided to see the school's guidance counselor to find some answers. The guidance counselor spoke to Jayden and realized that he might be suffering from depression. She referred him to a therapist to be evaluated.

Tori's story is a little different. Like Jayden, she was also more reserved, consequently, no one really noticed when she started withdrawing. She didn't feel like eating, so she started skipping meals. She got between two and four hours of sleep every night and felt completely drained all the time. Tori lost all interest in hanging out with her friends, schoolwork, and hobbies. She felt worthless and didn't want to burden others with her problems. Sometimes she would lash out at her parents for no apparent reason and they would make comments, such as, "Don't be so sensitive," or "Oh, she probably has PMS again." Every time she snapped at someone, she felt completely exhausted. Everything became a burden; even brushing her teeth would seem too much to handle. One day, she made a nasty comment to one of her friends. Her friend confronted her about it and asked her if she was going through something difficult because she changed over the previous few weeks. Tori confessed that she wasn't feeling herself and didn't understand what was going on with her. Her friend encouraged her to seek help.

Depression is a serious mental health disorder that can manifest in several ways. Sometimes, a specific event can trigger depression, and other times it sneaks up on you, nudging you to the edge until you have fallen into its pit.

WHY IS THIS HAPPENING, AND HOW DO I GET IT TO STOP?

Depression doesn't have one single cause. It can be caused by a whole list of things that are out of your control, including childhood trauma, a major life crisis, hormones, brain chemistry or biology, and genes. It can be triggered by one or a combination of these elements. Teens who have experienced some of the following triggers are more at risk for developing depression than others:

- A family history of depression.
- High levels of stress.
- Being abused or neglected.
- Physical or emotional trauma, such as being involved in a car accident or being bullied.
- Loss of a parent or other loved one.

- Chronic illness, such as cancer or diabetes.
- Traumatic brain injury.
- Other mental health issues, such as an eating disorder or anxiety.
- Loss of an important relationship, such as a close friend.
- Having a developmental or learning disorder.
- Substance abuse.

For instance, Tracy's depression most likely started as a result of the car accident that left her with many injuries and forced her to give up what she loved most; swimming. Cindy's depression, on the other hand, might have been caused by the fact that she was forced to take on mature responsibilities from a very young age. This can be traumatic for a young child. Her depression might also stem from her genetic makeup because her mother suffered from depression.

Now for the good news, the bad news, and everything in between. First, the bad news: There is no cure for depression. Just like you can't take a pill to miraculously heal diabetes, you can't cure depression. However, there is some good news: Depression can be treated and you can, together with a therapist, take back control of your life. In other words, we can't make depression go away for good, but we can learn how to deal with it. Depression usually occurs in episodes, meaning that its symptoms will make an appearance time and again. Learning how to recognize and deal with those symptoms can help you not to fall into the same pit. It is more than possible to be happy again and you can recover from depression. You just have to take that first step. Make an appointment with a trained professional to be properly diagnosed. Once you have been diagnosed, they can help you develop a treatment plan tailored specifically to your needs.

Treatment Options for Depression

Psychotherapy

Psychotherapy is probably the most popular and effective form of treatment for depression. It usually involves talking to a trained therapist who can help you to identify and replace negative thought patterns, explore relationships and build a support network, learn coping strategies, build confidence, and set realistic goals. Psychotherapy has been proven to be the best long-term form of treatment for depression. Keep in mind that you might need to visit a therapist or two before you find one that works best for you.

Medication

Remember, that there is no magic pill that can cure depression. However, sometimes, the chemicals in our brains need some help to balance themselves out. Psychiatrists normally prescribe antidepressants in extreme cases only, especially in teenagers. It is important to take these medications as recommended. It can be dangerous to increase or abruptly stop taking these medications without consulting your doctor. Be sure to speak to your doctor when you feel your depressive symptoms are getting worse. They might just need to adjust your dosage or prescribe a different antidepressant.

Lifestyle Changes

Certain lifestyle changes can also help you deal with depression. Examples include following a balanced diet, exercising, avoiding alcohol and substance abuse, taking supplements, such as vitamins and Omega-3s, and learning relaxation techniques. Self-care can also help you deal with depression. You can try a new hobby, draw a sketch, read a book, go on a hike, or simply take a long hot bath.

Build Your Support Network

We are social beings who need to connect with others despite what we might think or feel. Whether we are suffering from depression or not, we all need a support network to get through this difficult journey called life. Make sure that you have a support network that will be there to support you when you need it most. Your support network can be made up of friends, family, teachers, therapists, or neighbors. You can search for support groups in your area that are specifically for teenagers suffering from depression or you can join online communities. Just make sure that you are not alone in your journey to recovery.

CLINICAL CONFIRMATION

So, now you think you or a loved one might have depression. What should you do next? How can you or your loved one be diagnosed? The first thing you can do is visit your doctor. They can make sure that some of the symptoms you are experiencing are not caused by an underlying health concern. They will also do a screening. If they suspect that you might have depression, they will refer you to a therapist who will do a thorough evaluation by asking you certain questions. If they suspect that your symptoms might be caused by an underlying health issue, they might run some lab tests. They will also do a brief interview with your parents or caregivers about your behavior.

Remember not to take matters into your own hands by self-diagnosing and trying to treat your symptoms on your own. Doctors, therapists, psychologists, and psychiatrists have studied for years to diagnose and treat mental health disorders. The internet is not as reliable as you might realize, so be careful before you make a diagnosis.

Now that you know what depression is, let's talk about what depression is not.

NIP DEPRESSION IN THE BUD BY TAKING JUST ONE THOUGHT AND VIEWING IT THROUGH A NEW LENS

"Try to understand the blackness, lethargy, hopelessness, and loneliness they're going through. Be there for them when they come through the other side. It's hard to be a friend to someone who's depressed, but it is one of the kindest, noblest, and best things you will ever do."

— STEPHEN FRY

Everyone loves you when you're upbeat and positivity and humor flow—of course, being in a bright frame of mind is easier said than done, especially when you have depression.

If you are a teen with depression, then you know that one of the biggest problems is how misunderstood this disorder is. Most people think it involves feeling sad or being in a bad mood. When in fact, depression can make you feel numb, immobile, and frozen in the spot.

Imagine that you knew your favorite rock star was playing in your city this weekend, and you just couldn't muster up the energy to go. That's what depression does. It blocks out the things you most enjoy in life and leaves you devoid of energy.

It shoves you into a pit that can be damned hard to crawl out of.

Stephen Fry hit the nail on the head when he said that one of the kindest things you could ever do, is to be there for someone with depression.

If you really want to make a difference in their lives, one of the most valuable gifts you can share with them is information.

In the introduction to this book, I mentioned that we would be taking the proverbial depression monster by the horns through cognitive-behavioral therapy.

By understanding and reframing your thoughts, emotions, and behaviors, you can make major strides in your progress and curb an anxiety or depressive attack before it takes over your peace of mind.

Thankfully, we are living in an age in which talking about anxiety and depression is increasingly accepted. *Wednesday* star, Jenna Ortega, wrote a book sharing deeply personal stories about what it was like to struggle with mental health issues. Selena Gomez, meanwhile, has openly talked about how pushing yourself to the point of burnout can leave you with nothing left inside.

You may not have the extensive media access that these celebrities do, but you can let others know that sitting back and allowing depression and anxiety to take over is not their only option.

By leaving a review of this book on Amazon, you can motivate them to reframe their thoughts, manage and master their daily triggers, and develop strengths that will make them resilient against depression.

With just a few words, you can be the light someone needs to pull themselves out of a tunnel in which they have been passive observers of their life for too long.

Thank you for your help. A book is nothing without its readers.

Scan the QR code to leave a review!

5

COMMON MISCONCEPTIONS ABOUT ANXIETY AND DEPRESSION

> *Myths which are believed in tend to come true.*
>
> — GEORGE ORWELL

There are many myths about teenage mental health. What level of anxiety or unhappiness is considered to be normal? Are these emotions I'm experiencing just my hormones or am I really depressed? Maybe I won't feel so down if I get out more or make new friends. Or maybe I should just talk to a shrink. These are all questions and misconceptions teenagers have regarding mental health. If we are not careful, these and other myths can become part of our reality. So, to avoid being misled, we will debunk some common myths about teenage anxiety and depression.

MYTH 1: TEENAGERS DON'T ACTUALLY SUFFER FROM DEPRESSION AND ANXIETY, THEY JUST FEEL DOWN SOMETIMES

If only this was true. Unfortunately, mental health illnesses, such as anxiety and depression are more common among teenagers than we might expect. One study found that 3.2 million teenagers between the ages of 12 and 17 had one major depressive episode in 2017 (Brown, 2021). According to the World Health Organization (2021), the leading cause of illness and disabilities among teenagers are depression and anxiety and the fourth leading cause of death among young people is suicide.

MYTH 2: TREATMENT FOR ANXIETY AND DEPRESSION IS EASILY ACCESSIBLE

Many teens who show symptoms of depression and anxiety are not receiving treatment. According to Mental Health America, up to 60% of teens diagnosed with depression didn't receive treatment between 2017 and 2018 (Brown, 2021). Two-thirds of those who did decide to be treated for depression didn't continue receiving treatment consistently. It is important to receive consistent treatment to manage depression successfully. Without consistency, the likelihood of experiencing recurrent depressive episodes increases.

MYTH 3: DEPRESSION IS CAUSED BY AN UNSTABLE FAMILY

Although coming from a dysfunctional family may contribute to depression, it doesn't necessarily cause depression. Many teens come from highly unstable homes, yet they don't show any signs of depression or anxiety. While other teens come from "normal" or "healthy" families and still struggle with depression. Many factors play a role including, genes, family history of mental health disorder, trauma, major life events, and the list goes on. Depression can be caused by one or a combination of these factors.

MYTH 4: IF YOU HAVE ANXIETY, YOU WILL FALL APART AND WON'T BE ABLE TO ACHIEVE SUCCESS

Have you ever heard of high-functioning anxiety? Just because someone seems to cope well with their day-to-day tasks, doesn't mean they don't have anxiety. Don't judge a book by its cover. You might be an A-grade student, class president, and the most popular girl in school and still struggle with anxiety. No one will even notice your inner struggle because you have learned how to disguise it so well. Having high-functioning anxiety can be very frustrating because on the outside you seem fine, even great. Meanwhile, on the inside, you are freaking out.

What do individuals with high-functioning anxiety usually look like? Usually, they are driven, successful people, they arrive early, are always willing to help where they can, they are organized, proactive, passionate, outgoing, loyal, and appear to be quite calm. However, if you are able to have a look into their minds, you will find a completely different picture. Quite often, they are people-pleasers, afraid to disappoint or let others down. They lack boundaries, finding it difficult to say no. They are scared of what the future might hold. Their constant chatter might be a sign of nervousness. They sometimes have nervous habits, such as chewing their nails or pulling their hair. Insomnia is their friend because they tend to overthink and dwell on negative thoughts. Relaxing and enjoying the moment can be difficult for these individuals. They experience mental and physical fatigue. To cope, some resort to alcohol or substance abuse.

MYTH 5: ALL TEENAGERS EXPERIENCE DEPRESSION SOMETIME DURING ADOLESCENCE. IT IS JUST A PHASE.

Yes, there are many teens who silently suffer from depression, but not all teenagers do. Although it is important to reduce the stigma stuck to mental health disorders, we should not become desensitized. Depression during adolescence is not a normal part of growing up or "just a phase." It is a serious mental health condition that needs treatment. It is estimated that only one in ten individuals will experience a major depressive episode during their teenage years (Cheung, n.d.). It is interesting to note that girls are two times more likely to experience depression than boys (Brown, 2021). However, when their male peers do experience depression accompanied by suicidal thoughts, they are more likely to follow through with suicide (Cheung, n.d.).

MYTH 6: TECHNOLOGY CAUSES DEPRESSION AND ANXIETY

There are hundreds of articles flooding social media (ironic, don't you think?), warning us to switch off our phones because they are causing us to develop psychological problems. Although there might be a link between excessive use of social media and mental health disorders, it doesn't necessarily mean it is the cause of mental health disorders like depression. Sometimes the depression or anxiety was already there and social media is blamed to be the scapegoat. Smartphones, PCs, and PlayStations are often used by depressed or anxious individuals as a way to deflect their negative emotions and thoughts or simply to escape by mindlessly scrolling through social media or getting lost in video games. It is important to remember that although technology might not be a direct cause of a mental health disorder, resorting to social media or online gaming to help you cope with your symptoms, are not healthy. On the contrary, it can cause you to withdraw even more, aggravating your symptoms.

MYTH 7: SHE'S NOT DEPRESSED/ANXIOUS, SHE'S JUST LAZY.

No. She's not "just lazy." Both anxiety and depression can cause some serious fatigue. You might feel tired or sluggish all the time because both these mental health disorders can cause sleep problems. All those racing thoughts and overthinking can be extremely draining. Plus, chemical imbalances in the brain can contribute to low levels of motivation and energy.

MYTH 8: ALL ANXIETY IS BAD

We need anxiety to survive. If we didn't experience some level of fear, we would all be daredevils, hanging off of cliffs without any safety equipment. Many parents—and some teens today pathologize anxiety, thinking that every inconvenience contributes to anxiety disorders. There is a difference between experiencing anxiety and actually suffering from an anxiety disorder. If you failed a test, it is normal to feel anxious, seeing that we live in a competitive society and need good marks to get into college. The same is true for depression. Just because your boyfriend broke up and you feel heartbroken for a week or two, doesn't mean that you now suddenly have developed depression. Unfortunately, many parents today live in fear of their children developing some kind of mental health disorder so they call their therapist as soon as they experience a negative emotion. All emotions are good, even the not-so-nice-ones. They help us to become more resilient. However, they can become a problem when they start interfering with our everyday functioning.

MYTH 9: YOU CAN FIX YOUR ANXIETY WITH SOME COPING STRATEGIES

In some cases when you cut yourself with a knife, a band-aid will do. Other times, you might need a medical professional to stitch you up. The same is true for anxiety. Yes, there are some tips and tricks that you can use to help you cope with anxiety, but if you struggle with an actual anxiety disorder, you need professional treatment.

MYTH 10: YOUR PARENTS CAN MAKE YOUR ANXIETY GO AWAY, IF THEY WOULD JUST...

You or your parents can't make your anxiety go away by eliminating your stressors. School can be terrifying if you have an anxiety disorder, but enrolling you in an online school instead is not a healthy way to treat your anxiety. Having your mom sleep next to you because you can't sleep, will only enable your anxiety. You don't want to empower that monster that causes so much havoc in your mind. You want it to leave your thoughts. You can empower yourself by learning how to cope with your anxious thoughts and feelings. I am sure you and your parents just want to take it all away, but unfortunately, it doesn't work that way. Life is hard for all of us, so the best way to deal with anxiety is to learn coping strategies with the help of a therapist. Learning to fight back will take time, but it is worth it in the end. Take it from someone who has been there!

MYTH 11: YOU JUST HAVE TO FACE YOUR FEARS!

In some cases, facing our fears can help us overcome them. But if we—or our parents)—push ourselves too quickly, it can backfire. Treating anxiety disorders is much more complicated than simply confronting our fears—it takes a lot of support, time, and even more patience. Tackling small challenges equals big wins, so remember to take it one step at a time.

MYTH 12: YOU'RE JUST MANIPULATING YOUR PARENTS

Maybe you have heard this one before, "You're just lazy and don't want to go to school, stop trying to manipulate us," or "She cries about everything to get what she wants, she's not actually sad or depressed." Most people, teenagers and adults alike, are ashamed of their mental health disorder but will do almost anything not to feel the way they do. You are not manipulating your parents; you are just overwhelmed.

MYTH 13: HAVING ANXIETY OR DEPRESSION IS HOPELESS

The number 13 is believed to be the most dreaded number. Many people are superstitious on Friday the thirteenth to the point that some won't travel and others won't even go to work because they fear misfortune will find them. Even the hospitality industry is suspicious because some hotels don't have a thirteenth floor. The 13th person to show up at the Last Supper was Judas, the one who betrayed Jesus. Believe it or not, some people believe the opposite. In many eastern religions, this number is considered to bring fortune. Before the First World War, the number 13 was considered to be a lucky number in France.

Not one of these beliefs has scientific merit. However, if you suffer from anxiety or depression, there is hope. You don't have to dread your diagnosis like you might dread the number 13. Many treatment options are based on years of scientific research. You are fully capable of facing your condition and beating it and, if you are willing to give it a try, you can take control back of your life. The following chapters will focus on taking back that control, so, keep on reading!

6

TAKING CONTROL – COGNITIVE BEHAVIORAL THERAPY

> *You have considerable power to construct self-helping thoughts, feelings, and actions as well as to construct self-defeating behaviors. You have the ability, if you use it, to choose healthy instead of unhealthy thinking, feeling, and acting.*
>
> — ALBERT ELLIS

At the moment Cognitive Behavioral Therapy, or CBT for short, is known as the gold standard in the field of psychology. In other words, it is the best standard and has been proven to deliver the best results — it is the cream of the crop! CBT has proven over time to successfully treat depression and anxiety because it targets the core problem — those unhealthy thought patterns. In this chapter, we will have a look at all the ins and outs of CBT—what it is, how it works, why it works, and how it can be used to improve your thought life as well as your behavior and your overall well-being. Let's get going!

WHAT IS COGNITIVE BEHAVIORAL THERAPY?

CBT is based on both research and clinical practice. In other words, it not only looks good on paper, but it actually works in real life. It is a treatment method that focuses on regaining control over your thoughts. It focuses on two types of therapy—cognitive (your thoughts) and behavioral (your actions) therapy. As you might have noticed by now, when we experience stress, our bodies naturally react to combat that stress, which in turn causes a physical reaction. CBT is designed to help you reduce stress by focusing on your thoughts, thereby, minimizing those physical reactions and giving you back control.

CBT is based on the belief that how we think, feel and act are interconnected. What makes CBT so successful is that the therapist's goal is to help you become "your own therapist" by teaching you coping skills that you can use for the rest of your life. CBT teaches you to identify situations that trigger dysfunctional thought patterns, and how to cope with them. There are three basic principles CBT is based on:

- Unhealthy thought patterns are partially responsible for psychological problems.
- Learned patterns of dysfunctional behavior can contribute to psychological issues.
- Psychological problems can be reduced or even prevented by learning new thoughts and behavior patterns.

The big question is: How do we improve all those negative emotions that are all too common with anxiety and depression? Emotions are abstract and hard to control. By improving your thought-and-behavior patterns, your emotions will automatically improve. So, how does it work?

1. Recognizing Negative Thought Patterns

The first skill CBT focuses on is identifying negative thought patterns. This is often the most difficult part because it is difficult for most people, especially those with anxiety and depression, to engage in introspection. This is the first step on your road to self-discovery and recovery.

2. Practicing and Applying New Skills

The therapy room is a safe space to practice new skills before you apply them in the real world. Many therapists like to use role-play to help their clients gain self-confidence before going out in the world and using those new skills. For example, your therapist might present you with a certain anxiety-provoking situation, such as doing a class presentation. With the skills taught during your sessions, you now have the opportunity to practice your presentation in the safety of the therapy room. Before your presentation, you might do some breathing exercises, address some dysfunctional thought patterns and replace them with healthy and realistic thoughts and repeat a certain mantra. Your therapist will help you deal with those terrible triggers that seem to take over your life.

3. Setting Goals

What is the point of therapy if you don't have a goal to achieve? Together with your therapist, you will set both short-and long-term goals. This is an extremely important step in the recovery process. The focus should not only be on the end goal but also on the process. It is during the process that you start to heal and grow toward recovery. You will experience obstacles along the way, but you will learn how to cope with them. Remember, experience is the best teacher!

4. Problem-Solving Skills

Your therapist will help you to identify problems, create a list of possible solutions, identify the pros and cons of each, and finally choose and apply the preferred solution. Once you get the hang of this, you will easily be able to solve problems on your own. And when you need a bit of help, you can always contact your therapist for some advice.

5. Self-Monitoring

Self-monitoring involves keeping track of your thoughts, emotions, symptoms, experiences, and behaviors. This is usually done through journaling. This will help you and your therapist to keep track of and deal with negative thoughts and behavior patterns.

It is common for someone with an anxiety disorder to avoid their fears. CBT will help you to face your fears, instead of side-stepping them. You will feel more prepared when facing anxiety-provoking situations. It teaches you relaxation techniques that will calm both your mind and body.

CBT is not as intimidating as other forms of therapy might seem because the therapist and client work together as partners to solve problems. Although the therapist is the expert, they are not seen as superior to the client. The end goal is to help the client become their own "therapist." They become independent by learning how to identify and change their own thoughts, behaviors, and emotions.

HOW DOES CBT HELP WITH ANXIETY AND DEPRESSION?

CBT is not like other therapies that dig deep into the subconscious and require years or even decades of treatment to be effective. It is thought to be one of the most effective treatments for both anxiety and depression. Anxiety and depression are characterized by unrealistic and negative thought patterns. CBT will help you develop healthier, more realistic thought patterns. It is an effective short-term treatment that can be used to manage the symptoms of these mental health disorders. Therapy can take place either in the therapist's office or online in the comfort of your own home. This can be very helpful, especially for those who might be suffering from agoraphobia or panic attacks. CBT teaches you coping strategies that you can apply for the rest of your life. One can say that it is a short-term therapy that offers a long-term solution. That is if you choose to apply it in the long term.

It is based on a type of cognitive therapy, designed by Aaron Beck, developed especially to help treat anxiety and depression. Beck found that those clients who changed their dysfunctional thoughts to more realistic ones felt much better (Kaczkurkin & Foa, 2015). Once their thought patterns started to change, their emotions as well as their behavior improved. CBT is one of the most realistic therapeutic techniques because it teaches us that we can't control what happens around us. However, we have control over how we think, feel, and behave.

The most popular techniques used in CBT include (Raypole, 2022):

- Setting SMART goals—goals should be specific, measurable, achievable, realistic, and time-limited.
- Questioning and guided discovery—your therapist will challenge your negative thought patterns by questioning your assumptions and helping you discover different points of view.
- Journaling—this technique is used to identify and write down your negative assumptions and replace them with healthy, realistic ones. It

helps you to become aware of the underlying thoughts that influence your emotions and behavior. It also helps you to keep track of your progress and become aware of the thoughts that might contribute to your symptoms.
- Self-talk—much of what we think and feel comes from the way we talk to ourselves. Your therapist would teach you to identify some of those destructive conversations you have with yourself and how to replace them with positive, constructive self-talk.
- Cognitive restructuring—by identifying cognitive distortions, such as black-and-white thinking and jumping to conclusions, you can rewire your brain. This involves identifying and challenging negative assumptions. You look at your dysfunctional thoughts from different angles and evaluate whether or not they are indeed realistic. You then replace them with the truth. See the example below.
- Plan positive activities—you can plan a rewarding activity every day as a way of improving your mood. Activities can be anything from taking a bath to watching a movie.
- Situation exposure—this technique involves slowly exposing you to triggering events or

experiences. The goal is to desensitize you to such an extent that these events or experiences don't trigger you anymore.

- Behavioral activation—anxiety tends to lead us to avoid certain situations. This technique is specially designed to face those feared situations by deliberately scheduling them into our calendar. For example, if you are afraid to go to the mall because you might have a panic attack, you can schedule a coffee date with a friend and stick with it. Before your date, you can use relaxation techniques and do some positive self-talk.

- Exposure therapy—this technique is similar to situation exposure. It is often used to help individuals overcome their fears by gradually exposing them to a feared stimulus. By doing so, their negative assumptions about this stimulus are challenged and eventually replaced with a realistic belief. For example, you have a phobia of masses of water, such as pools and rivers. Your therapist might recommend that you start off dipping your toes in the pool, next you will stand on a step with the water up to your calves, then knee-deep, and so on. Finally, you will be able to stand on your tiptoes in the deep end without being afraid. By gradually exposing yourself to your fear, you challenge your irrational thoughts and in the process, you replace them with more realistic beliefs. Exposure therapy has been proven to be successful in treating PTSD, phobias, panic disorder, OCD, GAD, and social anxiety disorder.

Let's have a look at what cognitive restructuring might look like in a realistic situation.

Imagine you have a small class test coming up next week. You have a whole week to prepare for this test, yet you feel anxious and overwhelmed. You can't sleep, you withdraw completely and you are agitated most of the time. You haven't even looked at the chapter you are writing about. The first thing you have to do is to identify the negative thought that causes you to feel anxious. You might be thinking, "I am stupid and will fail this test."

After you have identified this negative thought, you have to challenge it. In the beginning, your therapist will help you to challenge this thought. After a while, you will get the hang of it and will be able to do this on your own. You can challenge your thought by looking for evidence for and against this assumption. The goal is to separate your feelings from reality. Remember, although emotions feel real and factual, they are abstract and mostly unrealistic. Just because you feel stupid, doesn't mean that you are stupid. You have made it through your entire school career until now, which means that you can't be stupid. Plus, you have an entire week to study for this test so you have more than enough time to prepare. You only have to study one chapter. So, think again; are your thoughts and feelings realistic? In CBT, you will probably discuss with your therapist why you feel stupid and overwhelmed.

The last thing you will do is replace your negative assumptions with positive realistic ones. The trick is not to lie to yourself, "I am going to study this chapter in one hour, I have nothing to worry about. I am going to get the best score in my class!" You have to be realistic; "Just because I feel overwhelmed and stupid, doesn't mean that it is true. I have made it this far. I have an entire week to study one chapter. If I study x number of pages every day, I will be able to get through all the work and pass this test."

CBT: BATTLING COGNITIVE DISTORTIONS WITH COGNITIVE INTERVENTIONS

Anxiety and Cognitive Distortions

In this section, we will have a closer look at what cognitive distortions are. We will also discuss some examples.

Simply put, cognitive distortions are negative thinking patterns that are false. It all has to do with how we perceive the world around us. The point of CBT is to correct these false perceptions and replace them with more realistic ones. Why do we develop cognitive distortions? To cope with negative life events of course. Forming cognitive distortions are part of our survival instinct, so they are not all bad. They are necessary for our immediate survival but can cause problems in the long term. They play a major role in anxiety and depressive disorders. Studies show that those with social anxiety have significantly more cognitive distortions than those who don't suffer from it (Erkan et al., 2017). They not only view themselves through negative lenses but also tend to judge others' behavior in a dysfunctional way. Let's look at a few examples of cognitive distortions with some examples:

Black-And-White Thinking

Also known as polarized or all-or-nothing thinking. You either assume the best or the worst, nothing in between.

Example: "If I don't get an A+ on the test, I am a complete failure."

Overgeneralization

You take one event and apply it to everything in your life.

Example: You have a misunderstanding with a friend about something insignificant, and now you assume that you are a bad friend.

Catastrophizing

This is when you assume the worst will happen without having any real evidence.

Example: "My mom is late to pick me up, something terrible must have happened, maybe she was in a car accident."

Personalization

This one is easy; taking things too personally. This usually happens when you blame yourself for things that are either out of your control or have nothing to do with you.

Example: While attending a party, your friends are busy talking to others. You immediately think that they don't want to talk to you or they suddenly don't like you. You feel like you don't belong.

Fortune Telling

You try to predict what will happen.

Example: You have a date; however, you predict that it won't turn out well. Your predictions are not based on factual evidence.

Should Statements

These are the things you tell yourself that you "should" or "ought to" do. You put unnecessary pressure on yourself, causing anxiety, frustration, guilt, and resentment.

Example: "I should lose more weight," or "I ought to study harder."

Emotional Reasoning

You assume that your emotions reflect your reality.

Example: You feel lonely because your friends are at a party. You assume that no one likes you or wants to be around you.

Labeling

Similar to overgeneralization, you take a single event as a basis for placing a label on yourself or others.

Example: You missed a goal at a football game, and now you label yourself as a bad player or a failure.

Control Fallacies

There are two types of control fallacies: external control fallacies and internal control fallacies. External control fallacies are when you believe that everything that happens to you is out of control, it must be fate.

Example: You believe that it is the teacher's fault that you failed the test, not because you didn't study.

Internal control fallacies are the complete opposite; you believe that you have complete control of yourself and your environment.

Example: Your beloved dog got sick. You feel guilty because you believe you should have watched what she ate, taken her temperature, and noticed she wasn't herself.

Filtering

This occurs when you "filter out" all the positive aspects of a situation and enlarge the negative aspects. You fail to see the silver lining because you focus on one negative piece of information.

Example: You received a B instead of an A for a particular assignment. You forget that you received A's for all your other assignments and choose to focus on this one. You feel like a failure because of this grade.

Cognitive Interventions

We are often unaware of what is really going on in our minds and how it affects our behavior and emotions. Over time, certain thoughts, whether they are positive or negative, are automatically generated and become part of our belief systems. Dysfunctional automatic thought patterns are also known as cognitive distortions (as discussed above). Cognitive interventions are a set of therapeutic techniques specifically designed to help us become aware of these automatic thoughts and find solutions for cognitive issues we might have. It is much more than "thinking positively." In fact, thinking positively sometimes causes us to live in denial. The main purpose of cognitive interventions is to identify, challenge and replace cognitive distortions. So, you can say that cognitive interventions are used to rewire your brain by changing your perspective. As a result, your thought patterns become more realistic, functional, and healthy. Your outlook on life becomes more positive without living in denial.

Anxiety is rooted in cognitive distortions. What you think influences your emotions and behavior. It becomes a vicious cycle, and avoidance behavior, which is typically associated with anxiety, only reinforces this cycle. For example, you think your friends don't like you, which makes you feel rejected, lonely, and sad. Consequently, when they invite you to hang out with them, you find an excuse and withdraw even more. This eventually becomes a pattern and, before you know it, you might even start avoiding going to school or having dinner with your family. Although avoidance behavior might seem like an easy solution for anxiety and depression, it only makes it worse. Clinical psychologist, Dr. Steven Lucerno believes that cognitive interventions are effective in breaking this cycle; "CBT helps individuals identify the links in the chain that lead to worse anxiety and depression: the thoughts, feelings, behaviors, and physical sensations that are intimately connected to one another" (Kerslake, 2021).

It is just as important to clean up our minds as it is to clean our bodies. When you are able to positively and realistically reframe your core beliefs, those feelings of anxiety and depression will decrease significantly. You are not denying your emotions or life's challenges; you are simply reframing your perspective by focusing on the facts and the here-and-now, instead of fixating on your emotions and stressing about what the future might hold. By replacing cognitive distortions with realistic beliefs, you can enjoy your relationships more, be more relaxed and be even more successful.

CBT IN ACTION

You don't have to wait to see a therapist to apply certain CBT techniques to help you cope with anxiety and depression. You can start today! However, it is still very important to schedule an appointment with a therapist to be diagnosed and receive the correct treatment.

Journaling

One of the most effective tools therapists recommend is journaling. You can start by writing down your thoughts and feelings. This will help you to identify cognitive distortions and how they influence your emotions and behavior. If writing is not your thing, you can try vlogging. Push that record button and start talking about your day, what happened, how it made you feel, what thoughts popped up in your head throughout the day, and how you reacted. Later on, you can listen to yourself, identify negative thoughts, challenge them, and replace them with more realistic ones. You can even record the new thoughts over the old ones. The point of journaling is to become aware of your thoughts and how they affect your everyday functioning.

Exposure Therapy

To overcome some of your fears, you can try to do some exposure therapy. It is important to take small steps. If you feel uncomfortable hanging out in groups, start small. First, make plans to hang out with one friend at home. Next week, try to hang out with two friends. The week after, arrange to meet three friends at the mall, and so on. The important thing is to stick with your plans. By gradually exposing yourself to social situations, your brain starts to realize that hanging out with friends doesn't put your life in danger. Slowly you become desensitized.

Activity Scheduling

This technique is especially helpful if you suffer from depression. One of the most known symptoms of depression is a loss of interest in things that you used to enjoy. Activity scheduling involves planning these types of activities. Let's say before you started feeling depressed, you loved to paint or go on hikes. Make sure to schedule a specific time in your day or week to fill a blank canvas or to go hiking. If you enjoy reading, set time apart every day to read at least one chapter.

Incorporating CBT techniques in your day doesn't have to be rocket science. The trick is to take it one day at a time. Don't fixate on the past or focus on the future. Instead, try to be present in the here and now. Remember not to be too hard on yourself. Your symptoms won't improve overnight, so be patient.

In the next chapter, we will have a look at the power of our thoughts and how dangerous negative thought patterns really can be!

7

TAKING CONTROL–THE POWER OF YOUR THOUGHTS

> *I want to teach people around this country that the happier you are, the healthier you are, and the more sleep that you get, the more successful you can be.*
>
> — KAMRIN BAKER

These are the words of 17-year-old Kamrin Baker who has been diagnosed with an anxiety disorder. She understands that happiness starts within so she started the Joy is Genius Campaign (JIG) which is specifically designed by teenagers for teenagers to help them cope (Baker, 2014). If you are able to change your mindset, you will be happier and healthier. In this chapter, we will have a closer look at the power of our thoughts and how they can either help us to grow or deteriorate.

MINDSET MATTERS: FIXED VS. GROWTH

Your mindset is a set of beliefs you have that influence how you view yourself and the world around you. Your beliefs are like a pair of glasses—if your lenses are rose-colored, everything around you will look rose-colored. If your lenses are dark, the world around you will appear dark. Your mindset affects how you think, feel and behave. Most importantly, it determines how you see yourself and is responsible for your success or failure.

There are two kinds of mindset—a fixed mindset and a growth mindset. If you have a fixed mindset, you believe that your traits can't be changed. When you have a fixed mindset, you can't achieve your full potential, and here's why:

- You believe that you were born a certain way and there's nothing you can do about it—there is no room for growth or improvement.
- You tend to avoid challenges and give up easily if you encounter obstacles.

- Putting in the effort to achieve something seems futile and you feel threatened by others' success.
- You avoid any form of criticism—whether it is positive or negative.
- You feel that whatever happens to you is part of your fate.
- You see trials and tribulations as a sign to give up rather than as an opportunity to grow.

On the other hand, if you have a growth mindset, you empower yourself because:

- You believe that there is always room for growth.
- Anything can be improved if you put effort into it.
- You can develop your abilities, learn new skills, and change your outlook on life.
- You believe that you are a work in progress and are able to evolve to adapt to your surroundings.
- You embrace challenges and don't back down when you face setbacks.
- You don't see criticism as the enemy but rather use it to improve.

- You are not intimidated by others' success but draw inspiration from it.
- You believe that you have free will and can take control of your own actions, thoughts, and feelings.

Let's have a look at a practical example. You failed a math test. If you have a fixed mindset, you would think, "I was never good at math anyway." You accept the fact that you are not born with the ability to do math and you don't find ways to improve your score for the next test. But if you have a growth mindset you would look at the mistakes you made, learn from them, and take control. You might get a tutor and put in more effort to score better next time.

THE POWER OF A GROWTH MINDSET

Part of your mindset is about how you view yourself—are you intelligent, capable, and talented, or are you average, powerless, and unqualified? This has a significant effect on how you feel about yourself and how you behave. Studies suggest that your mindset is so important, that it can determine your success or your failure. In a particular study, researchers found that junior high students showed increased motivation and performed better after being taught about a growth mindset

(Smith, 2020). Another study showed that those students who had a growth mindset performed better in mathematics and language and had a higher grade point average (GPA) than those students who had a fixed mindset (Smith 2020). In a 2018 study, research showed that students in the United States with a growth mindset scored 60 points higher in reading than those with a fixed mindset (Sparks, 2021).

If you have a growth mindset, you don't allow your past to determine your future, you are able to learn new skills, and take your future into your own hands. The world becomes your oyster as you don't limit yourself to your present abilities. It also promotes resilience so you will be able to face life's challenges and bounce back when you experience hardships.

Have you heard of experience-dependent neuroplasticity? Well, if you haven't then you are in luck, you are about to now! Science proves that your brain is capable of changing. You are not doomed to your fate; you can improve and take back control of your life. Experience-dependent neuroplasticity proves that experiences can change the brain. Our brains are made up of billions of neurons that all work together and are responsible for all of our experiences, such as sleeping, eating, falling in love, and learning. Every time you have an experience, the connections between these neurons become stronger, and the more you have a certain experience, the more these connections are reinforced. As a result, that particular part of the brain becomes more active and thus stronger. The opposite is also true—when we don't have a certain experience often, those neurons become weaker and eventually wither away. So, what does this mean for anxiety and depression? The more you experience fear, hopelessness, and helplessness, the stronger these feelings become. However, the more you are able to identify, challenge and replace those negative thoughts, the weaker they become. The key is deliberately focusing on planning and implementing positive experiences, repetition, and a whole lot of patience. I am sure you know the alphabet by heart. This is not because you were born with this knowledge, it is because you repeated the alphabet throughout your childhood, whether you repetitively recited it in class or sang the alphabet song over and over again. The point is, repetition can change the way your brain works. Once that loneliness strikes, think back to a positive memory with friends or reach out to a loved one. Change your focus and soon your thoughts, feelings, and behavior will follow. This reminds me of a well-known proverb by Sitting Bull: "Inside of me there are two dogs. One is mean and evil and the other is good and they fight each other all the time. When asked which one wins, I answer, "the one I feed the most" (Sitting Bull, 2023).

Another phenomenon that proves the importance of mindset, is the placebo effect. In a certain study, researchers found that if they told participants they were consuming a caffeinated drink, their blood pressure would rise even though the drink didn't contain any caffeine (Collins, 2018). If your thoughts can have this impact on your physical health, imagine what it can do for your mental health!

YOUR THOUGHTS INFLUENCE YOUR SURROUNDINGS

Your mindset determines how you cope with life's challenges. With all the evidence supporting the power of your thoughts on your physical and mental well-being, can you see how important it is to be aware of your thoughts? Your brain is constantly changing to adapt to your surroundings, whether you are aware of it or not. This is why you have to be hyper-vigilant about what is going on in your thoughts. If you are not aware of what is going on in your brain, your environment will shape it for you. By consciously focusing on certain activities and strengthening those positive neural pathways, you can change the way your brain works. You won't see the results immediately because it will take some time to weaken those cognitive distortions and create new, realistic ones. Keep on monitoring, challenging, and changing those negative thought patterns. If you are patient, your symptoms will improve over time and you will live a happier, healthier life. Focus on the journey, rather than the end goal and challenge yourself to improve. Don't allow your past or fate to define you; start developing a growth mindset today.

HACKS TO TRICK YOUR BODY INTO HAPPINESS

Did you know that you can actually trick your body into happiness and relaxation? The human body is a wonderful thing. It produces many chemicals that can alter your mood. If you understand how these chemicals work, you can do certain things to trick your body and mind into happiness. In this section, we will have a look at four happy hormones—dopamine, oxytocin, serotonin, and endorphins.

Dopamine

Dopamine is a feel-good hormone that is linked to your brain's reward system. Once your body releases dopamine, the body experiences feelings of pleasure which motivates you to repeat a certain behavior. It, therefore, plays an important role in motivation. Depression and anxiety are accompanied by low levels of dopamine. But there is good news! Foods that increase dopamine levels include:

- eggs
- walnuts
- almonds
- fatty acids from fish like salmon, mackerel, and tuna
- apples
- avocados
- leafy green vegetables
- dairy
- sesame and pumpkin seeds
- unprocessed lean meat

You can give your body a little boost to produce more dopamine by:

- Exercising
- Listening to music
- Getting some sunlight
- Meditating
- Consuming probiotics
- Getting a massage
- Taking a cold shower

Serotonin

This hormone regulates your mood and plays a role in sleep, appetite, memory, digestion, and learning. Interestingly, your gut is responsible for producing serotonin. Therefore, following a well-balanced diet and eating gut-friendly foods will promote the production of this hormone. These foods include:

- eggs
- salmon
- cheese
- dark chocolate
- poultry
- spinach
- seeds
- milk
- soy products
- nuts

Other ways you can boost serotonin production include:

- Getting exercise
- Spending time with animals
- Keeping a gratitude journal
- Taking a warm bath

- Aromatherapy
- Reducing stress
- Socializing
- Helping others
- Laughing
- Spending some time in nature

Oxytocin

This hormone is also known as the love hormone because it plays a role in bonding and promotes trust and empathy. Hugging, touching, and cuddling all produce oxytocin. It plays an important role in mood regulation. You can just imagine, if you feel loved and wanted and bonded with a friend or even a pet, your mood will automatically improve. Foods that will boost oxytocin production include:

- avocados
- figs
- spinach
- green tea
- watermelon
- orange juice
- broccoli
- dark chocolate
- extra virgin olive oil

- chia seeds
- chamomile tea

Here are some additional ways to increase the production of oxytocin:

- Doing some yoga
- Listening to music
- Getting a massage
- Sharing your feelings with a loved one
- Spending time with friends
- Meditating
- Actively listening to others
- Cooking with a loved one
- Doing something nice for someone
- Petting your dog or cat

Endorphins

Endorphins are your body's natural pain reliever in response to stress and also plays a role in experiencing pleasure. The body naturally produces endorphins when we get injured, experience stress, or when we engage in rewarding activities. Endorphin-producing food includes:

- Apples
- Bananas
- Asparagus
- Beans
- Berries
- Coffee
- Brown rice
- Dark chocolate
- Eggs
- Ginseng
- Grapes
- Green tea

You can naturally increase endorphin production by:

- Exercising
- Meditating
- Aromatherapy
- Laughing with friends
- Watching a dramatic series or movie
- Making music
- Being kind to someone
- Catching some sunshine
- Taking a hot bath

KAMRIN'S STORY

Let's quickly go back to Kamrin's story. Kamrin was able to manage her anxiety on her own. It wasn't until her panic attacks took over her life that she realized something had to change. She wanted to experience the zest of life and be a beacon of hope to others. She deserves more than being a victim of her anxiety disorder. She decided that she didn't want to miss out on another day. The thing with anxiety is that you don't plan on missing out; life happens and anxiety happens. The difference is her perspective; she picks herself up every day, even if it takes an hour to gather her strength. Although she still struggles with anxiety, her strong mindset and stubborn will doesn't allow her to become stuck in the claws of her mental health disorder. She constantly has to tell herself: "This isn't me. I am strong. Life is good." She knows that her anxiety disorder doesn't define who she is. She realizes the importance of her perspective in keeping her anxiety disorder in check, even though she experienced many panic attacks in her life. Kamrin understands that having a growth mindset is the most effective way to beat anxiety. Be smart. Be like Kamrin.

Before we are going to learn about triggers, let's just quickly recap the difference between a fixed and a growth mindset. A fixed mindset is narrow-minded—

you believe that you are born a certain way and you can't improve. You don't put in any energy to improve yourself because you believe your efforts will be futile. Criticism is your enemy and you avoid it at all costs. A growth mindset is the opposite—you believe that you can improve when you put in some effort. You learn from others' success and don't feel intimidated by it. You are humble and use criticism to improve yourself. A growth mindset has been proven to improve anxiety and depression, just look at Kamrin's story!

8

TAKING CONTROL–MANAGING AND MASTERING DAILY TRIGGERS

Addressing anxiety is very important and different for us all. I explain to clients that we all experience anxiety; however, it is how we deal with the stress that can help." –Dr. Rufus Tony Spann

Each individual is unique—not one person on this planet experiences life in the same way. How we experience and deal with anxiety is no different. Your triggers will be completely different from the triggers of the person next to you. This is why it is important to be able to identify and deal with your triggers. In this chapter, we will learn almost everything there is to know about triggers—what they are, common triggers, how to identify them, and how to deal with them.

UNDERSTANDING AND IDENTIFYING TRIGGERS

What Are Triggers?

Triggers set off an alarm, causing you to feel anxious or depressed. Triggers are the things that activate your symptoms and can be anything from emotions to events and experiences. Identifying triggers is the most important step in learning how to manage them. For example, if you have a fear of rejection, a typical trigger would be a friend who doesn't reply to a text message immediately. Instead of thinking that they might be busy, you immediately feel that they are angry with you or you irritate them. This triggers you to feel rejected.

Common Triggers

Although our experiences may be unique, there are certain triggers that individuals with anxiety and depression share.

Social Situations

This is probably one of the most common triggers. This can range from public speaking and hanging out in groups to the fear of leaving the comfort of your home. Those suffering from panic attacks or agoraphobia tend to avoid social situations at all costs. Anxiety and depression have a way of making us feel self-conscious and not good enough.

Medications

Certain medications, such as steroids, stimulants, and decongestants can trigger feelings of anxiety because they influence the brain's chemistry. If this is the case, you can always make an appointment with your doctor who can prescribe an alternative.

Caffeine

This might be surprising, but consuming too much caffeine can aggravate anxiety symptoms. Maybe you are ingesting too much caffeine and don't even realize it. Remember that in addition to coffee, certain carbonated drinks and chocolate also have high amounts of caffeine. If you suspect that your coffee, cold drink, or chocolate addiction might worsen your anxiety, maybe it is time to start weaning yourself off and rather choose healthier alternatives.

Sleep

Not getting enough sleep can make you feel more anxious or even depressed. Sleep deprivation can have you stuck in a never-ending cycle—you feel anxious or depressed because of lack of sleep, these feelings cause your mind to race, especially at night, causing you to sleep even less and therefore increasing your anxiety or depression, and so the cycle continues. If this is the case, consider creating a relaxing bedtime routine. Cut out caffeine late in the day. Try to eliminate screen time before bed because the light of the screen prevents your body from producing enough melatonin, the sleep-inducing hormone.

Stress

One of the most common triggers of anxiety is stress. Usually, once a stressful event passes, it goes away. However, if you have an anxiety disorder, this might not be the case. Stress intensifies anxiety, even when the stressor is no longer present. The best way to deal with stress is to try and eliminate as many stressors as possible. Unfortunately, we can't remove all stressors from our lives, but we can learn to cope with them. If you need help, ask. If you have a big test coming up, create a study schedule and stick to it. If you feel stressed do some breathing exercises.

Relational Conflict

Whether you argue with a friend or whether your parents are fighting at home, relational conflict can be a major trigger. It can leave you feeling frustrated and trigger anxious thoughts and feelings. Talking to a trusted friend or even better, talking to a therapist will help you deal with these frustrations.

Major Life Transitions

Moving to a new city, attending a new school, having newly divorced parents, or losing a loved one can trigger anxiety and depression. Not all transitions are negative. However, even the positive ones, such as entering the exciting new world of college, can cause a great amount of stress and anxiety. Take active steps in planning how you will handle the new transition. If you need a bit of help, talk to a loved one or a therapist.

Being Bullied

Bullying can be a major trigger for both anxiety and depression. It can take place online or in real-life social situations, such as at school. Being bullied can make you feel anxious to go to school and in some cases, it can spill over into other social situations where the bully is not even present.

Food

Believe it or not, skipping meals can trigger anxiety. When you skip a meal, your blood sugar levels will drop, which causes your body to go into fight-or-flight mode. This can make you feel nervous, have sweaty, shaky hands and have a grumbling tummy. These symptoms can trigger anxiety because they imitate anxiety symptoms. You can help keep your blood sugar levels stable by eating regular healthy snacks.

Similarly, having an unhealthy diet can also trigger anxiety. Research shows that individuals with a diet high in processed carbohydrates are more at risk for developing anxiety than those who have a healthy and balanced diet (Murphy, 2022). The reason for this is that processed carbohydrates cause major fluctuations in blood sugar levels. So next time you want to grab that big bag of chips, rather settle for an unprocessed alternative, such as whole wheat products or fresh fruit and vegetables.

Social Media

According to a certain study, excessive social media use can be associated with an increased risk of anxiety (Murphy, 2022). Social media can be triggering for several reasons:

- Pressure to conform to unrealistic standards and expectations.
- Reading about the news.
- Cyberbullying.
- Information overload.

You don't necessarily have to get rid of all your social media platforms. The trick is to find a balance. It is very easy to get swept up in the infinite universe of TikTok for an hour or two. Try to limit yourself by not checking those social media platforms every ten minutes.

Specific Phobias

There are five main categories of phobias:

- Fear of animals, for example, spiders, dogs, or snakes.
- Fear of specific situations, for instance, driving, elevators, or small spaces.
- Fear of blood or anything that pierces the body, such as surgery or needles.
- Fear of natural environments, for instance, water, heights, or thunderstorms.
- Other phobias that don't fall under the above-mentioned categories.

How Do I Know What My Triggers Are?

Now for the important part: identifying triggers. Perhaps you already know what your triggers are. If you do, keep on reading because this section will help you to confirm your triggers and maybe you might even discover new ones.

Why is it important to know what your triggers are? Because if you know where your anxiety comes from, you will be able to manage it better. The physical symptoms of anxiety can be overwhelming, often causing you to overlook the root cause of your symptoms. Think of a tree, if you just cut off the branches, the tree will just grow again. In most cases, it will grow even better than it did before you trimmed the branches because the roots will become stronger. The only way to get rid of the tree is to take out its roots. Think of triggers as roots. To help you cope with your anxiety, it is important to identify triggers and understand why they make you feel anxious. For example, if you become very anxious when you are about to take a test, then taking a test is the trigger. Now you have to determine why this is so triggering. Maybe you feel inadequate or you are afraid of failing. Once you have determined the root cause and the reason for the trigger, you can think of solutions to help you deal with the underlying fear.

Seeing a therapist for an evaluation is an important step in identifying your triggers. Recognizing your triggers might become easier once you know what type of anxiety you have. For example, if you are diagnosed with social anxiety, you will have a better understanding of where your anxiety comes from—social situations.

It is important to understand the symptoms of anxiety in order to recognize your triggers. Research shows that those individuals who kept a journal where they recorded their symptoms and experiences, were better able to avoid relapses (Gussone, 2021).

Identifying your triggers is a huge step toward healing. You can do this on your own, however, professional guidance is highly recommended. A therapist will diagnose you and help you narrow down and confirm possible triggers, making the process quicker and much more bearable.

COPING SKILLS AND MANAGEMENT METHODS

Can I Just Avoid My Triggers?

You might think avoiding your triggers is a viable long-term solution. Unfortunately, this is not the case. It might be effective in the short term but it is not sustainable to avoid your triggers all the time. Avoidance behavior reinforces negative thoughts, feelings, and behaviors. So, avoiding triggers can do more harm than good. An effective way of overcoming avoidance behavior is to do the exact opposite: exposure therapy. Let's recap what exposure therapy is all about by looking at an example:

Imagine you just had a panic attack at the mall. After this experience, you developed a fear of going there because you are afraid it might trigger another panic attack. As a result, you now avoid going to the mall at all costs. In the short term, this might be a reasonable solution; however, you can't avoid the mall forever because someday you will need something that you can only find there. To overcome this, you can try some exposure therapy. First, you can drive past the mall. The following week, you can drive to the mall and sit in the car in the parking lot for a few minutes. Next, you can decide on walking to the entrance and then entering the mall. Finally, you can arrange to meet a friend there and hang out. Taking small, baby steps and being patient with yourself are important when overcoming avoidance behavior.

Another reason why avoiding triggers is not effective is because it is unrealistic. Some triggers can subtly trigger feelings of anxiety, such as low blood sugar levels, caffeine, or the news. It is virtually impossible to avoid all triggers. This is why it is important to learn coping and management skills to deal with the side effects of depression and anxiety.

Healthy Coping and Management Mechanisms

Recognizing your triggers is already a healthy management technique. Knowing what you're up against can help you to make healthy, informed decisions in coping with anxiety and depression. In this section, we will have a look at some healthy management techniques and coping strategies that you can use to manage your symptoms.

Grounding Techniques

1. The 5, 4, 3, 2, 1 Method

This method is effective because it interrupts those intrusive thoughts and distracts you from some of the symptoms. In this exercise, you are going to engage all your senses—sight, hearing, touch, smell, and taste. You are going to find:

- Five things you can see—a blue car, a large tree, or an old book.
- Four things you can touch—a rusty pole, a smooth tabletop, or a fluffy pillow.
- Three things you can hear—cars driving past, birds chirping outside, or a plane flying over the house.

- Two things you can smell—soap, coffee, or freshly cut grass.
- One thing you can taste—a mint, a sip of juice, or a pinch of salt.

That's it! You simply use your surroundings to ground yourself. Try to take in every sensory experience as much as possible. Notice the distinct textures, colors, sizes, loudness, and tastes of everything you observe.

2. Engage Your Senses

This is very similar to the technique mentioned above. Do something to engage your senses. For example, pet your dog. While petting your dog, notice the texture and color of its fur. Take in the scent of your beloved pet and listen to the noises it makes while you are cuddling it. Try to engage as many senses as possible. Another example is to become a tree hugger. Yes, a tree hugger. If you are near a park or garden, you can take off your shoes. Feel the texture of the grass underneath your toes. Take slow, deep breaths. Take in the scent of the fresh air. Go to the nearest tree and touch it. Feel the roughness (or smoothness) of the tree bark. Close your eyes and listen to the noises of nature—the birds singing, a dog barking, the wind blowing through the leaves.

3. Feel Your Body

With this technique, you consciously become aware of how your body feels. Start with your head and end with your toes. Is your hair tied up or can you feel your hair touching your shoulders? Feel the weight and texture of your shirt on your shoulders. Are your shoulders shrugged or relaxed? What is the position of your arms? Notice the pace of your breathing and heart rate. Are you hungry or full? What are your legs doing? What is the position of your feet? Feel the weight of your shoes on your feet. If you are barefoot, become aware of the surface beneath your feet. Are your toes relaxed or curled up? Try to notice how every inch of your body feels.

De-Stressing Techniques

1. Setting Boundaries

A very important skill to learn that will help you in all areas of your life is setting healthy boundaries. The point of a boundary is to keep whatever is inside its walls safe by keeping danger out. You need to protect yourself against unnecessary stress and sometimes that means saying no. Most of us are people-pleasers—we overcommit to keep those around us happy causing us great amounts of stress. Saying no is not always easy, but it is necessary to stay sane. Be warned that most people don't respond well when we start setting boundaries. They might get angry or feel confused because they are not used to you saying no. In the beginning, it will be very difficult, but as you practice setting healthy boundaries, you will feel less stressed and more in control of your life. If you don't know how to set healthy boundaries, do some research, or even better, talk to your therapist. They will help you to define healthy boundaries and address misconceptions about others' perceptions of your new skill.

2. Delegate

Try to break big tasks into smaller, more manageable steps. Use a journal or calendar to plan your week. For example, if you have a big test coming up next week, break the work down into smaller parts. Study five to ten pages every day instead of cramming in all the work two days before the test. Breaking up the study material into more manageable parts, will give you enough time to thoroughly prepare and even do some revision the day before the test.

Long-Term Management Techniques

1. Create a Balanced Lifestyle

As you know by now, an unbalanced diet, inadequate sleep, and unhealthy lifestyle choices can all contribute to anxiety and depression. Be sure to follow a balanced diet. To keep your blood sugar levels in check, try to snack regularly. Get enough sleep by minimizing screen time, set up a schedule so that you don't have to do chores or homework late at night, go outside and catch some sunshine during the day to boost your melatonin (sleep hormone) production at night, and cut out caffeine late at night. Getting enough exercise will also boost your overall well-being and help you sleep better. And remember to schedule some "me-time" every day where you take time for yourself to do whatever makes you feel good and relax.

2. Schedule Worry Time

This might seem a bit unconventional but research shows that setting some time apart to worry can improve sleep and reduce negative thoughts (Starr, 2022). Start by setting aside 20 minutes every day. If you want to start your day stress-free, schedule your worry time early in the morning. If you want to wind down by clearing your head before bed, plan it during the evening. Whenever these fears come up during the day (believe me, they will!), acknowledge them briefly and then set them aside for your scheduled worry time. By taking some time every day to worry, your mind will eventually realize that whatever you are worrying about is not urgent. You will feel that you have more control over your concerns.

For more coping and healthy management strategies refer back to chapter 2 and chapter 3. Remember that it is important to recognize and learn how to deal with your triggers. Avoiding them can cause even more problems, aggravating your depression and anxiety. Face them head-on and talk to a therapist to help you manage them. The next chapter will focus on developing your strengths.

TAKING CONTROL–DEVELOPING YOUR STRENGTHS

> *When our brain continues to feel that we're in danger when we're not, that stress starts to create all kinds of physical and emotional problems. Having a toolbox of different techniques ready to go when you realize you're stressed is really important."*
>
> — DR. DEBRA KISSEN

Identifying and developing your strengths is one of the most important tools in your toolbox of healthy management strategies. Doing what you love and learning a new skill is the perfect medicine for a discouraged heart. It combats stress and releases all kinds of feel-good hormones that will improve your mood and alleviate anxiety.

FIGHTING ANXIETY WITH ACTION

A certain study found that taking time every day to engage in a creative activity can lead to improved psychological well-being (Schild, 2020). Adopting a new hobby or learning a new skill will help you de-stress, vent some of your negative emotions, calm your mind, boost your self-confidence, and finally alleviate some of your anxiety. One study showed that 75% of individuals who participated in a creative activity had lower levels of the stress hormone cortisol (Parkhurst, 2021). Engaging in activities you love won't completely resolve your anxiety and depression, but will help to relieve some of the symptoms. However, if you combine healthy activities with therapy, medication if necessary—and self-care, you have a recipe for success.

Psychologist and author, Dr. Michael Yapko (2018, p.) states: "Many of the triggers for depression are the painful things that happen in our relationships–the betrayals, humiliations, rejections, and abandonments. The skills necessary to build and maintain healthy, enduring relationships are on the decline." You can combat depression by learning how to nurture, re-establish or create new social connections. By engaging in enjoyable activities, you can build new friendships and enhance old ones, while building a healthy support network that will help you through life's challenges. Research showed that individuals who participate in a team sport or hobby regularly are less likely to show symptoms of depression, anxiety, or stress (Parkhurst, 2021).

HOBBIES AND SKILLS TO COPE WITH ANXIETY

Certain hobbies and skills are very effective in relieving symptoms of anxiety. Here is a list of some activities you can try:

Become a Chef

Cooking a delicious meal or baking a tasty treat can be very rewarding. Try to engage all your senses while cooking or baking. Feel the texture of the ingredients, smell the aromas, and don't forget to do a taste test once in a while. Not only can you enjoy the fruit of your labor, but you can share it with your loved ones. If you don't know how to cook, it is never too late to learn. There are plenty of recipes available online, including videos that show you how to create a delicious meal, step-by-step.

Dust Off Those Gardening Gloves

Gardening is not only relaxing but the whole process can be satisfying, and the result is very rewarding. Getting outside and catching some sun boosts your mood and produces vitamin D which is good for your health. A change of scenery distracts you from your worries and surrounding yourself with beauty can relieve some of your symptoms. Plant some flowers, herbs, or vegetables and enjoy the process of watching them grow. Pick the flowers and put them in your room or use the fresh ingredients in your cooking. You don't have to have a massive garden. If planting from scratch seems like too much effort, you can always get some indoor plants to nurture.

Try to Do Some Calligraphy or Modern Hand-Lettering

You can use this new skill to write a note to a friend, make study notes, write in your journal, or simply just for fun. There are plenty of YouTube videos which you can learn and draw inspiration from.

Get Some Fish

Maintaining an aquarium holds many health benefits, including decreasing blood pressure and relieving stress. Although you might not think so, taking care of an aquarium is a creative activity because you have the opportunity to create something unique. You can design your own little underwater world in the comfort of your own home by creating a mix of plant life, rocks, and fish.

Get a Massage

Studies show that when we get a massage, whether we do it ourselves or someone else does it for us, the receptors in our skin signals our brain that it is safe to relax (Dolgoff, 2020). You don't have to get a professional masseuse; you can do it yourself. Try to focus on those tense spots on your body, such as your neck, shoulders, feet, and hands. You can also use this as a grounding exercise by taking in the aroma of the oil, feeling its warmth between your hands, and feeling the relief as those tight muscles become looser.

Dance Your Stress Away

Not only will you get some exercise, but you will also notice that your stress will melt away. Dancing has many advantages while listening and dancing to happy music can trigger positive memories, making you feel good. It also engages the mind and brings on inspiration. There is no need to join a class or to even dance in front of others. You can simply close your door, put on some upbeat music, and dance the night (or day) away!

Knit a Scarf

No, knitting is not only for your grandma or older people. It is a creative skill that has many advantages. As you know by now, engaging in a creative activity can relieve symptoms of anxiety and depression. There is scientific evidence that the repetitive nature of knitting is calming and meditative (Dolgoff, 2020). Another study showed that women suffering from an eating disorder who knit experience less anxiety than those who didn't knit (Dolgoff, 2020). If you don't know where to begin, attend a knitting class or go to the store or library and get a book that shows you how to knit. A more convenient option is to search DIY knitting videos online that will show you how to knit, step-by-step.

The list of hobbies and activities that you can choose from is endless. The most important thing is to make time to do something you enjoy. The more creative, the better.

BAND-AID SOLUTIONS

Eat Some Sauerkraut

According to a study published by Psychiatry Research, individuals diagnosed with social anxiety who ate one serving of fermented food daily were more outgoing in social settings than those who didn't eat any fermented foods (Hilton Anderson, 2017). Sauerkraut and other fermented foods, such as yogurt, kefir, and kimchi, contain good bacteria that are important for a healthy gut.

Cuddle a Furry Friend

The National Institute of Health found that having an animal as a companion reduces social anxiety (Hilton Anderson, 2017). You don't have to get a dog or cat, even a scaly friend, such as a lizard will do.

Be Kind

In a study published by Motivation and Emotion, researchers found that small acts of kindness have been found to reduce social anxiety (Hilton Anderson, 2017). When we are kind to others, our focus shifts from our own worries to others' feelings which gives us a sense of purpose. So, next time your mom is cooking dinner, give her a helping hand.

Self-Care

It is very important to take care of your physical, emotional, mental, and spiritual well-being. To do this, you have to deliberately set time aside every day for some self-care. Having some well-deserved me-time will re-energize your mind, soul, and body. Even if it is just 15 minutes a day, make sure you make time for yourself every single day.

Clean Your Room

Did you know that cleaning your room can be good for your health? There are many health benefits associated with keeping your room clean. Have you ever noticed that if your room is a mess, you tend to feel more stressed and overwhelmed? Cleaning your room can provide you with a sense of order and control. A 2017 study found that clutter was associated with procrastination, lower quality of life, and feeling overwhelmed (Silva, 2022). Familiarity and consistency help us to feel safe and secure. Physically cleaning your room will help your body to produce endorphins which will help to relieve stress, reduce pain, and improve your overall well-being. Having a clean room will decrease unnecessary distractions and improve your focus.

Have a Cup of Tea

According to a study conducted by the University College of London, having a cup of tea can help you recover more quickly from everyday stress. Those who had four cups of black tea a day for six weeks were found to have decreased levels of cortisol (Hallett, 2018).

Chew Some Gum

A particular study presented at the International Congress of Behavioral Medicine shows that chewing gum can relieve anxiety, reduce stress, and improve alertness (Hallett, 2018). Next time you are feeling stressed, take out a packet of gum and start chewing!

Visit an Art Gallery

Not all of us are born with an artistic flair. Rest assured; you don't have to be an artist to relieve some stress. Studies have found that simply looking at art can lower your anxiety levels (Hallett, 2018).

Take a Nap

Researchers have found that taking a short nap can improve your immune system, relieve stress, and combat the negative effects of a poor night's sleep (Hallett, 2018). So, when insomnia comes knocking on your door, be sure to take a short nap the following day to relieve some stress.

What hobbies and activities do you enjoy? Are there any listed in this chapter that you enjoy doing? If not, maybe it is time to try something new. In the final chapter, we will look at some resources you can turn to when you are feeling overwhelmed.

10

TAKING CONTROL–YOU'RE NOT ALONE

> *Never just give up on a person with anxiety.*
>
> — ERIN WHITTEN

Heather was born a worrier. Since she could remember, she would worry about the most insignificant things. She thought everyone experienced these feelings but as she got older, she realized that her loved ones didn't share her concerns.

Heather always had an open relationship with her parents, however, when it came to her anxiety, she would rather sugar-coat the truth than be completely honest with them. She didn't want to burden them with her trivial problems. They noticed something was off and sent her to a therapist who diagnosed her with generalized anxiety disorder. She received medication and some counseling. Her parents were very supportive but she still didn't want to cause them unnecessary concern.

After receiving therapy, she still struggled with anxiety. Soon she started showing signs of depression and she fell into a deep hole of despair and inner turmoil. Soon she started getting thoughts of self-harm and she even started cutting herself. One night her brother almost walked in on her while she hurt herself. She felt so ashamed and decided to tell her dad what she was going through. He reassured her that they will get through her depression together.

One day she attended a concert with her friends. Heather also struggled with social anxiety so this was a big step for her. Somehow during the concert, she got separated from her friends, which brought on a panic attack. Luckily, one of her friends found her and helped her through the panic attack. Afterward, Heather confided in her friend who offered her support.

Heather never knew her loved ones could be so understanding, supportive and patient. If only she talked to them sooner.

Learning how to cope with anxiety and depression can be overwhelming but you don't have to do it alone.

Heather tried to hide her anxiety and depression from her loved ones. This only increased her symptoms and only once she confided in those she loved and trusted, could she receive the love and support she deserved. There are places you can turn to for some support. This chapter is dedicated to providing you with resources you can turn to for some extra support, so try as many as possible and stick with those that work best for you.

ONLINE THERAPY

Online therapy is a convenient alternative to face-to-face therapy. It comes in many forms, including online video calls, text messages, or even emails. There are many online support groups you can join as well as skill-building programs that are specifically designed to empower those who are diagnosed with depression and anxiety. Whether you decide to go with online or face-to-face therapy, be sure to check the therapist's credentials.

GROUP COUNSELING SESSIONS

Research shows that group therapy is effective in decreasing depression among teenage girls (Javanmiri et al., 2013). Teenagers naturally relate to their peers. Attending group therapy will provide you with companionship, you will realize that you are not alone and that others share your struggles. Finally, you will feel understood and group therapy will teach you to trust others. It is also an effective way of learning social skills in a safe space, which can be especially helpful if you struggle with social anxiety.

MEDITATION AND MENTAL HEALTH APPS

It is impossible to visit your therapist every time you are about to experience a panic attack or you feel the depression is about to sink in. There are many apps available that can help you keep track of your thoughts and feelings and set goals and reminders. Some of these apps even offer professional advice and are completely anonymous. Others are based on CBT principles which will help you in your journey to healing. There are also many apps available that will teach you relaxation techniques and guide you through meditation.

TIKTOK

Many of us turn to social media for advice. TikTok is an easy platform to access when you need advice. Many trained professionals offer hacks on TikTok that can help relieve symptoms of anxiety. Use this platform with caution as many individuals offer advice that is not research-based. Before trying out some of these hacks do some additional research and contact your doctor or therapist to confirm that it is safe to use.

LIGHT THERAPY LAMPS

Light therapy lamps are often used to treat depression. Being exposed to light is important to regulate your sleep-wake cycle. If you don't catch enough sun rays, your body will not produce enough melatonin, which is important to induce sleep. Light therapy lamps will help reset your internal clock by increasing your serotonin levels by day and your melatonin levels by night. Improved sleep results in an improved mood. Light therapy lamps are usually used early in the morning for 30 minutes at a time. Consult your doctor before using a light therapy lamp.

FOOD

Certain foods can boost your mood and help relieve your anxiety:

- Dark leafy greens, such as spinach and kale—fight inflammation.
- Avocado—contains oleic acid which is important for brain function.

- Walnuts—full of depression-fighting omega-3 fatty acids.
- Mushrooms—lower blood sugar levels and promote a healthy gut.
- Berries—packed with antioxidants.
- Beans—stabilize blood sugar levels.
- Onions—contain anti-inflammatory properties and antioxidants.
- Tomatoes—contain folic acid and alpha-lipoic acid which is effective in fighting depression.
- Seeds—rich in omega-3 fatty acids.
- Apples –are full of antioxidants and fiber to keep blood sugar levels stable.

Don't use this list as an excuse to binge. These foods can help relieve feelings of depression by incorporating them into your diet in a balanced way.

AROMATHERAPY AND ESSENTIAL OILS

Essential oils are widely used to relieve anxiety, improve mood, and help individuals unwind. You can throw a few drops into your bath or massage your skin with it. Take time to really take in the aroma of essential oils. Certain essential oil blends are specifically combined to combat feelings of anxiety and depression.

Others are blended to increase alertness and concentration.

FIDGET TOYS

Fidget toys are designed to help relieve anxiety. It can assist in relieving symptoms of stress, anxiety, OCD, and ADHD. It increases attention and concentration and can serve as a healthy distraction from your negative thought patterns. Popular fidget toys include fidget spinners, fidget cubes, chewable jewelry, keychains, and kneadable doughs.

WEIGHTED BLANKETS

Many people swear by the amazing power of weighted blankets. They usually weigh between four and thirty pounds and offer pressure stimulation which simulates being hugged. This pressure can release dopamine and serotonin and combat anxiety and depression. It has a grounding effect that lowers cortisol levels, thus calming the body's fight-or-flight response to stress. This sensation is effective in relieving anxiety and insomnia.

ADULT COLORING BOOK

Coloring is not just for preschoolers. Many adults use adult coloring books as a way to relax and unwind, especially after a long day. A study conducted in 2017 found that female university students who colored daily for a week reported decreased feelings of anxiety and depression compared to the beginning of the study (Santos-Longhurst, 2022). Researchers suspect that the colors and the act of coloring itself have a calming effect. Coloring is a great distraction and gives your brain a break from all those intruding thoughts. It helps you to be present in the moment and therefore improves concentration. Some people even use coloring as part of their bedtime routine.

FRIENDS

Positive friendships are associated with greater well-being because it creates a sense of belonging and boosts your self-esteem. Having a friend to talk to when you are feeling stressed can help you cope with your anxiety. Sometimes you just need a hug. Receiving a hug has been found to relieve negative emotions (Salinas et al., 2021). Having friends also promotes healthy choices. For example, if you have a friend who loves engaging in physical activities, you might end up joining them for a hike one day. Good friends are also honest and have your best interests at heart so they won't be afraid to call you out on your unhealthy behavior.

MENTAL HEALTH COUNSELOR

The most recommended treatment for depression and anxiety is seeing a therapist. Mental health professionals are trained to assess, diagnose and treat mental health disorders and many counselors specialize in teenage anxiety and depression. They will offer you relationship advice and help you navigate through life's challenges. You can ask your doctor to refer you to a counselor or simply search for therapists online. Sometimes you have to try on a few shoes before you get the perfect fit. The same is true when finding a therapist. You might not get along well with the first therapist you make an appointment with. Don't give up; continue searching for a therapist who will meet your unique needs.

ERIN'S STORY

Erin never understood what anxiety was about until one of her closest friends started to suffer from severe anxiety. She realized that anxiety is much more than feeling nervous all the time. Her friend's anxiety was so severe that he couldn't leave the house some days. He experienced panic attacks that lasted for almost an hour and some days he couldn't even get out of bed.

Erin took it upon herself to help him. Unfortunately, this made her feel helpless because she felt her efforts were futile. She realized that the best thing she could do for him is just to be there when he needed her and not give up on him. Although she can't stop the panic attacks or take away the intrusive thoughts, she can support him and listen to him when he needs to talk.

There are people out there like Erin who are more than willing to help those suffering from anxiety or depression. Not because they can get something out of it, but simply because they care. You too can find such a friend. Don't be afraid or ashamed to reach out for help, whether it is to a trusted friend, family member, or therapist. Make sure that you have a support system that will be there when life's pressures seem to overwhelm you.

HELP SOMEONE ELSE TAKE CONTROL OF THEIR THOUGHTS AND EMOTIONS AND KNOW THEY ARE NOT ALONE.

As you start applying the useful strategies contained in this book, you may feel more like sharing your new sense of confidence and empowerment with others readers.

Simply by leaving a review of this book on Amazon, you will help other teens see life through a more positive lens, so they can embrace thoughts and emotions that lead to optimal behaviors.

Thank you for your help. Together, we can help others master their triggers, act instead of react, and embrace the healing therapies and approaches that help them achieve their individual goals.

Scan the QR code to leave a review!

CONCLUSION

Both anxiety and depression can leave you feeling lonely and misunderstood. It is not just a phase you have to go through as a teenager. Although you are experiencing many changes, constantly feeling anxious or depressed is not normal. Don't be afraid to reach out for help.

Anxiety is characterized by intense concern about the future and causes avoidance behavior and a whole list of physical symptoms. It can be caused by genetics, trauma, or other external factors such as the pandemic or social media. There are different anxiety disorders, including generalized anxiety disorder, social anxiety disorder, obsessive-compulsive disorder, panic disorder, separation anxiety, and post-traumatic stress disorder. Although you can self-diagnose, it is recommended that you get diagnosed by a trained professional. A misdiagnosis can do more harm than good. So be sure to make an appointment with a therapist before you start any kind of self-treatment.

Panic attacks are quite common among people with anxiety disorders. They are different from anxiety attacks in that they are more intense and mostly appear out of the blue. They are accompanied by severe physical symptoms. Anxiety attacks are usually expected and last much longer.

Depression is associated with feelings of hopelessness and loss of interest in previously enjoyed activities. It is more than feeling a little blue on a rainy day—it is an intense, overwhelming feeling that takes over your entire life. Everyone's experience of depression is different, some feel sad all the time while others constantly seem angry. Like anxiety, it can be caused by genes, stress, or trauma. Other causes include the loss of a loved one, illness, developmental disorders, and substance abuse.

CBT is one of the most effective therapeutic techniques for anxiety and depression. The power of the mind is incredible; it can determine your success or your failure. CBT techniques are specifically developed to change negative thought patterns into more realistic positive ones. This therapeutic intervention will empower you, help you to take control back of your life, and is a helpful tool for developing a growth mindset.

An important part of treating anxiety and depression is recognizing your triggers. Knowing your triggers can help you to cope with your anxiety or depression and is a big step towards your recovery. Avoiding your triggers can aggravate your symptoms, trapping you in a never-ending cycle, which is why it is important to learn how to deal with them. Effective CBT techniques that rule out avoidance behavior are exposure therapy, grounding techniques, engaging your senses, and de-stressing strategies.

Hobbies and engaging in other activities can also help you cope with your symptoms. Although this is not a cure, it can alleviate some of the symptoms. Activities such as cooking, gardening, knitting, and dancing have many benefits for your physical and psychological well-being.

Remember that negative emotions are not bad—they are there for a reason, and they send us a message that something is not right. So, when you find your emotions spiraling, take a deep breath and listen to your body and mind. Identify your negative thoughts, challenge them, and replace them with realistic positive ones.

Just because you have anxiety or depression, doesn't mean your life is over. Unfortunately, there is no quick fix but you can learn how to manage and cope with your symptoms. Through CBT, therapy, and other coping strategies discussed in this book, you will be happy again. You will have a fulfilling and meaningful life.

Remember Kamrin's story in Chapter 7? You can also learn how to deal with your mental health disorder and take charge of your life just like her. It might take some effort and a whole lot of patience, but you will get there. Her strong mindset helped her to overcome her anxiety. Her determination even led her to help other teens suffering from mental health disorders. It is time to get your life back on track. If Kamrin can do it, so can you!

Did you find this book helpful? If so, don't hesitate to leave a review.

REFERENCES

A, K. (2012, February 29). *"I became so depressed that I stopped going to school."* HuffPost. https://www.huffpost.com/entry/teen-depression-i-became_n_1309913

Abraham, M. (2020a, October 10). *How Anxiety Toys With Your Emotions.* Calm Clinic. https://www.calmclinic.com/anxiety/anxiety-emotions

Abraham, M. (2020b, October 10). *Unusual ways that anxiety affects behavior.* Calm Clinic. https://www.calmclinic.com/anxiety/symptoms/behavior

Ackerman, C. (2017, September 29). *Cognitive distortions: twenty-two examples and worksheets.* PositivePsychology.com. https://positivepsychology.com/cognitive-distortions/

Adcock, D. (2022, February 4). *Ten hobbies that help fight depression and anxiety.* The Source. https://www.thesource.org/post/10-hobbies-that-fight-depression-anxiety

Alban, D. (2022, June 8). *How to Increase Dopamine Naturally.* Be Brain Fit. https://bebrainfit.com/increase-dopamine/

Alyssa. (2022, March 29). *Dopamine foods: Boosting your mood naturally.* Banyan Treatment Center. https://www.banyantreatmentcenter.com/2022/03/29/dopamine-foods-boosting-your-mood-naturally-massachussetts/

American Psychological Association. (2017, July). *What is cognitive behavioral therapy?* https://www.apa.org/ptsd-guideline/patients-and-families/cognitive-behavioral

American Psychological Association. (2022, August). *Anxiety.* https://www.apa.org/topics/anxiety

Ankrom, S. (2022, August 24). *What happens during an anxiety attack.* Verywell Mind. https://www.verywellmind.com/what-is-an-anxiety-attack-2584253

Anxiety and Depression Association of America. (2022, December 12).

A teen's story. Anxiety and Depression Association of America. https://adaa.org/living-with-anxiety/personal-stories/teens-story

Arlin Cuncic. (2022, November 6). *The characteristics of high functioning anxiety.* Verywell Mind. https://www.verywellmind.com/what-is-high-functioning-anxiety-4140198

Bailey, E. (2010, September 7). *What is "fight or flight" and how does it relate to anxiety?* Health Central. https://www.healthcentral.com/article/what-is-fight-or-flight-and-how-does-it-relate-to-anxiety

Baker, K. (2014, April 8). *"My anxiety does not define me."* HuffPost. https://www.huffpost.com/entry/teen-anxiety-story_b_5106252

Baker, K. (2017, December 6). *I'm 17 with an anxiety disorder--and I deserve better.* HuffPost. https://www.huffpost.com/entry/im-17-with-an-anxiety-disorder-and-i-deserve-better_b_6906818

Bennett, C. (2018, July 31). *Health anxiety and dangers of self-diagnosis.* News-Medical.net. https://www.news-medical.net/health/Health-Anxiety-and-Dangers-of-Self-Diagnosis.aspx

Bettino, K. (2021, March 12). *What to know about teenage depression.* Psych Central. https://psychcentral.com/lib/teenage-depression#symptoms

Binu, S. (2022, April 3). *Oxytocin: Foods that boost your love hormone.* Netmeds. https://www.netmeds.com/health-library/post/oxytocin-foods-that-boost-your-love-hormone

Bissell, J. (2019, June 28). *Eight quick anxiety hacks experts recommend when you feel overwhelmed.* Bustle. https://www.bustle.com/p/how-to-calm-down-anxiety-with-these-8-quick-hacks-18156077

Brandt, A. (2019, June 3). Three steps to treat your anxiety using CBT. Psychology Today. https://www.psychologytoday.com/us/blog/mindful-anger/201906/3-steps-treat-your-anxiety-using-cbt

Brown, M. (2021, May 9). *Teenage depression: facts and statistics.* Psych Central. https://psychcentral.com/depression/teenage-depression-facts

Bruce, D. F. (2022, April 24). *Teen depression.* WebMD. https://www.webmd.com/depression/guide/teen-depression

Carter, S. M. (202 C.E., January). *Best Meditation Apps Of 2022.* Forbes

Health. https://www.forbes.com/health/mind/best-meditation-apps/

Cassata, C. (2021, March 23). *Here's the verdict on TikTok's most popular anxiety hacks.* Verywell Mind. https://www.verywellmind.com/the-verdict-on-tiktok-s-most-popular-anxiety-hacks-5116715

Cherney, K. (2020, August 25). *Effects of anxiety on the body.* Healthline. https://www.healthline.com/health/anxiety/effects-on-body

Cherry, K. (2022a, August 10). *What is cognitive behavioral therapy?* Verywell Mind. https://www.verywellmind.com/what-is-cognitive-behavior-therapy-2795747

Cherry, K. (2022b, September 20). *What is a mindset and why it matters.* Verywell Mind. https://www.verywellmind.com/what-is-a-mindset-2795025

Cheung, A. (n.d.). *Teenage depression: Separating myth from reality.* RBC Children's Mental Health Project. http://www.rbc.com/donations/pdf/Teenage-Depression-Separating-Myth-from-Reality.pdf

Clayton, V. (2021, September 8). *Ten common depression symptoms.* Forbes Health. https://www.forbes.com/health/mind/common-depression-symptoms/

Coelho, S. (2020, June 11). *Anxiety disorders: Types, causes, and symptoms.* Medical News Today. https://www.medicalnewstoday.com/articles/types-of-anxiety

Cognitive behavioral therapy quotes. (n.d.). Goodreads. https://www.goodreads.com/quotes/tag/cognitive-behavioral-therapy

Collins, N. (2018, June 13). *How the human mind shapes reality.* Stanford News. https://news.stanford.edu/2018/06/11/four-ways-human-mind-shapes-reality/

Cuncic, A. (2022, October 19). *How to increase serotonin.* Verywell Mind. https://www.verywellmind.com/how-to-increase-serotonin-5248440

Curtiss, J. E., Levine, D. S., Ander, I., & Baker, A. W. (2021). Cognitive-behavioral treatments for anxiety and stress-related disorders. *FOCUS, 19*(2), 184–189. https://doi.org/10.1176/appi.focus.20200045

David, D., Cristea, I., & Hofmann, S. G. (2018). Why cognitive behavioral therapy is the current gold standard of psychotherapy. *Frontiers in Psychiatry, 9*(4), 1–3. https://doi.org/10.3389/fpsyt.2018.00004

Davis, K., & Sissons, B. (2023, January 6). *Anxiety attack: Symptoms, causes, and complications.* Medical News Today. https://www.medicalnewstoday.com/articles/307863

Davis, S. (2022, May 31). *How five mental health experts alleviate their own anxiety.* Forbes Health. https://www.forbes.com/health/mind/mental-health-experts-anxiety-tips/

Davis, V. (2021, February 19). *Anxiety triggers: How to identify and overcome them.* Hims. https://www.forhims.com/blog/common-anxiety-triggers

Dekin, S. (2021, November 22). *Teenage anxiety on the rise: what's contributing to this problem?* Mission Harbor Behavioral Health. https://sbtreatment.com/blog/teenage-anxiety-on-the-rise-whats-contributing-to-this-problem/

DeMarco, C. (2022, February 9). *Seven anxiety hacks: How to manage stress and worry in the moment.* MD Anderson Cancer Center. https://www.mdanderson.org/cancerwise/anxiety-hacks--7-tools-to-manage-stress-and-worry-in-the-moment.h00-159537378.html

Dolgoff, S. (2020, May 1). *Fifteen stress-reducing activities you can do at home.* The American Institute of Stress. https://www.stress.org/15-stress-reducing-activities-you-can-do-at-home-according-to-experts

Duszynski-Goodman, L. (2022, December 6). *What does a mental health counselor do?* Forbes Health. https://www.forbes.com/health/mind/what-is-a-mental-health-counselor/

Erkan, K., Safak, Y., Ozdemir, I., & Tulaci, R. G. (2017). Cognitive distortions in patients with social anxiety disorder: Comparison of a clinical group and healthy controls. European *Journal of Psychiatry, 32*(2), 97–104. https://doi.org/10.1016/j.ejpsy.2017.08.004

Farnam Street Media. (2023). *Carol Dweck: A summary of the two mindsets.* Farnam Street. https://fs.blog/carol-dweck-mindset/

Felman, A. (2020, September 7). *Social anxiety disorder: Causes, symptoms, and treatment.* Medical News Today. https://www.medicalnewstoday.com/articles/176891#what-is-it

Ferguson, S., & Casabianca, S. S. (2021, May 5). *Anxiety in children: signs and symptoms to look for.* Psych Central. https://psychcentral.com/anxiety/symptoms-anxiety-children-teens#social-anxiety

Foran, C. (2019, April 16). *Six cognitive distortions that could be fueling your anxious thoughts.* Health.com. https://www.health.com/condition/anxiety/cognitive-distortions

Fredericks, K. (2021, January 11). *Ten tips for understanding and managing anxiety and panic disorder.* The Healthy. https://www.thehealthy.com/mental-health/anxiety/manage-anxiety-and-panic-disorder/

Friedman, R. A. (2018, September 7). *The big myth about teenage anxiety.* The New York Times. https://www.nytimes.com/2018/09/07/opinion/sunday/teenager-anxiety-phones-social-media.html

George Orwell quotes. (n.d.). Brainy Quote. https://www.brainyquote.com/quotes/george_orwell_377904

Gholipour, B. (2016, March 22). *Even more evidence that anxiety can be genetic.* HuffPost. https://www.huffpost.com/entry/even-more-evidence-anxiety-can-be-biological_n_56f17b4ee4b03a640a6bd967

Goodyear, S. (2014, October 6). *What it's like to be in high school with an anxiety disorder.* HuffPost. https://www.huffpost.com/entry/teen-anxiety-disorder_b_5938538

Gotter, A. (2019, December 5). *Racing thoughts: tips for coping.* Healthline. https://www.healthline.com/health/racing-thoughts

Grothaus, M. (2014, December 1). *Take two apps and call me in the morning.* Fast Company. https://www.fastcompany.com/3039100/take-two-apps-and-call-me-in-the-morning

Gussone, F. (2021, June 10). *Anxiety triggers: How to spot and overcome them.* Ro. https://ro.co/health-guide/anxiety-triggers/

Guzman, S. (2023a, January 11). *What Is Anxiety? Symptoms, Causes And Treatments.* Forbes Health. https://www.forbes.com/health/mind/what-is-anxiety/

Guzman, S. (2023b, January 24). *What is a panic attack? Symptoms, causes and remedies*. Forbes Health. https://www.forbes.com/health/mind/what-is-a-panic-attack/

Hallett, R. (2018, January 12). *Eleven activities to ease anxiety and stress that are totally free*. Women's Health. https://www.womenshealthmag.com/uk/health/mental-health/a704353/11-free-activities-to-ease-anxiety/

Harness, J., & Javankbakht, A. (2021, June). *Trauma*. Anxiety and Depression Association of America. https://adaa.org/understanding-anxiety/trauma#What%20is%20trauma?

Harvard Health Publishing. (2020, August 1). *Recognizing and easing the physical symptoms of anxiety*. Harvard Health. https://www.health.harvard.edu/mind-and-mood/recognizing-and-easing-the-physical-symptoms-of-anxiety

Hasan, S. (2018). *Anxiety disorders*. Kidshealth.org. https://kidshealth.org/en/parents/anxiety-disorders.html

Haseltine, W. A. (2021, August 25). *Depression and anxiety double in youth compared to pre-pandemic*. Forbes. https://www.forbes.com/sites/williamhaseltine/2021/08/25/depression-and-anxiety-double-in-youth-compared-to-pre-pandemic/?sh=3bf33e60139f

Herndon, J., & Raypole, C. (2022, January 28). *Is there a "cure" for depression?* Healthline. https://www.healthline.com/health/can-you-cure-depression

Higuera, V. (2021, November 1). *Everything you need to know about depression*. Healthline. https://www.healthline.com/health/depression#symptoms

Hilton Anderson, C. (2017, February 9). *Nix social anxiety: Eleven tricks to calm down your mind*. The Healthy. https://www.thehealthy.com/mental-health/anxiety/social-anxiety-tips/

Holland, K. (2022, September 29). *What triggers anxiety? Eleven causes that may surprise you*. Healthline. https://www.healthline.com/health/anxiety/anxiety-triggers#triggers

Holland, M. (2023, January 25). *Seventeen common anxiety triggers and how to cope with them*. Choosing Therapy. https://www.choosingtherapy.com/anxiety-triggers/

Hurley, K. (2021, February 25). *Six hidden signs of teen anxiety*. Psycom. https://www.psycom.net/hidden-signs-teen-anxiety

I was weighed down by depression and didn't ask for help. (2019, May 26). Your Teen Magazine. https://yourteenmag.com/health/teenager-mental-health/teen-depression-and-anxiety

Ismail, N. (2022, December 20). *High-functioning anxiety: Symptoms, causes and treatment*. Forbes Health. https://www.forbes.com/health/mind/what-is-high-functioning-anxiety/

Ismail, N. (2023, February 20). *Your guide to the best light therapy lamps*. Forbes Health. https://www.forbes.com/health/mind/best-light-therapy-lamps/

Jameson, E. (2014, March 2). *This is what depression really feels like*. HuffPost. https://www.huffpost.com/entry/teen-depression_b_4518746

Javanmiri, L., Kimiaee, S. A., & Abadi, B. A. G. H. (2013). The study of solution-focused group counseling in decreasing depression among teenage girls. International Journal of *Psychological Studies, 5*(1). https://doi.org/10.5539/ijps.v5n1p105

Johnson, B. (2014, May 27). *Stop an anxiety attack in five simple steps*. Lifehack. https://www.lifehack.org/articles/lifestyle/stop-anxiety-attack-5-simple-steps.html

Jowaheer, R., & Savin, J. (2022, January 14). *Twenty-one anxiety relievers to help you feel calmer*. Cosmopolitan. https://www.cosmopolitan.com/uk/body/health/g32010556/anxiety-products/

Joy, K. (2017, January 11). *Panic attack vs anxiety attack: Six things to know*. The University of Michigan. https://healthblog.uofmhealth.org/wellness-prevention/panic-attack-vs-anxiety-attack-6-things-to-know

Julson, E. (2022, March 1). *Ten best ways to increase dopamine levels naturally*. Healthline. https://www.healthline.com/nutrition/how-to-increase-dopamine

Kaczkurkin, A. N., & Foa, E. B. (2015). Cognitive-behavioral therapy for anxiety disorders: an update on the empirical evidence. *Dialogues in Clinical Neuroscience, 17*(3), 337–346. ncbi. https://doi.org/10.31887/DCNS.2015.17.3/akaczkurkin

Kerslake, R. (2021, September 19). *Everything you need to know about cognitive behavioral therapy for anxiety*. Healthline. https://www.healthline.com/health/anxiety/cbt-for-anxiety#cbt-for-anxiety

Lawler, M. (2021a, August 2). *Why friendships are so important for health and well-being*. Everyday Health. https://www.everydayhealth.com/emotional-health/social-support.aspx

Lawler, M. (2021b, August 25). *Why friendships are so important for health and wellbeing*. Everyday Health. https://www.everydayhealth.com/emotional-health/social-support.aspx

Legg, T. J. (2019, August 22). *What can trigger anxiety?* Medical News Today. https://www.medicalnewstoday.com/articles/326134#being-bullied

Leonard, J. (2019, September 23). *Generalized anxiety disorder (GAD): Symptoms, causes, and treatments*. Medical News Today. https://www.medicalnewstoday.com/articles/326416

Leonard, J. (2021, January 21). *Differentiating between panic and anxiety attacks*. Medical News Today. https://www.medicalnewstoday.com/articles/321798#differences

.Leonard, J. (2022, April 22). *Symptoms, signs, and side effects of anxiety*. Medical News Today. https://www.medicalnewstoday.com/articles/322510#diagnosis

Lester, J. (2023, January 31). *Eight pieces of expert advice for mental health*. Forbes Health. https://www.forbes.com/health/mind/expert-advice-for-mental-health/

Lindberg, S. (2021, April 9). *What are the different types of anxiety?* Healthline. https://www.healthline.com/health/anxiety/types-of-anxiety#diagnosis

Marais, S. D. (2022, August 2). *Five practices for calming racing thoughts*. Psych Central. https://psychcentral.com/health/how-to-calm-racing-thoughts#healthy-distractions

Mass General Brigham McLean. (2021, July 10). *Panic attacks: recognizing one and what to do*. https://www.mcleanhospital.org/essential/panic-attacks-recognizing-one-and-what-do

Mayo Clinic. (2018, February 3). *Depression (major depressive disorder)*.

https://www.mayoclinic.org/diseases-conditions/depression/diagnosis-treatment/drc-20356013

Mayo Clinic. (2020, June 6). *Countdown to make anxiety blast off.* Mayo Clinic Health System. https://www.mayoclinichealthsystem.org/hometown-health/speaking-of-health/5-4-3-2-1-countdown-to-make-anxiety-blast-off

McLean Hospital. (2022, March 20). *Panic and anxiety: do you know the difference?* Mass General Brigham McLean. https://www.mcleanhospital.org/essential/panic-anxiety-difference

MD, P. G. (2022, May 4). *How to recognize and tame your cognitive distortions.* Harvard Health. https://www.health.harvard.edu/blog/how-to-recognize-and-tame-your-cognitive-distortions-202205042738

Medline Plus. (2022, December 14). *Teen depression.* https://medlineplus.gov/teendepression.html

Meijia, Z. (2022, June 27). *What is cognitive behavioral therapy?* Forbes Health. https://www.forbes.com/health/mind/what-is-cognitive-behavioral-therapy/

Menasce Horowitz, J., Graf, N., Parker, K., & Horowitz, J. (2019). *Most U.S. teens see anxiety and depression as a major problem among their peers.* https://www.pewresearch.org/social-trends/wp-content/uploads/sites/3/2019/02/Pew-Research-Center_Teens-Report_FINAL-1.pdf

Mental Health America. (2022). *Is depression curable?* Mental Health America. https://screening.mhanational.org/content/depression-curable/?layout=actions_a

Michelson, A. (2021, September 28). *Sucking on sour candy may help calm your next panic attack, according to a therapist.* Insider. https://www.insider.com/how-sour-candy-may-calm-your-next-panic-attack-therapist-2021-9

Miller, C. (n.d.). *Depression and anger.* Child Mind Institute. https://childmind.org/article/depression-and-anger/

Miller, C. (2022, August 17). *How anxiety leads to disruptive behavior.* Child Mind Institute. https://childmind.org/article/how-anxiety-leads-to-disruptive-behavior/

Miller, C. (2023, January 5). *How anxiety affects teenagers.* Child Mind

Institute. https://childmind.org/article/signs-of-anxiety-in-teenagers/#symptoms-of-anxiety-in-teenagers

Miller, L. (2023). *Debunking myths of teen depression*. Johns Hopkins Medicine. https://www.hopkinsmedicine.org/health/wellness-and-prevention/debunking-myths-of-teen-depression

Minnicks, M. (2022, May 9). *Twenty-five endorphin-releasing foods and beverages that may make you happier*. CalorieBee. https://caloriebee.com/diets/25-Endorphin-Releasing-Foods-and-Beverages-That-Make-You-Happy

Molineux, A. (2022, May 31). *The health risks of self-diagnosing mental disorders*. News-Medical.net. https://www.news-medical.net/health/The-Health-Risks-of-Self-Diagnosing-Mental-Disorders.aspx

Murphy, C. (2022, August 19). *Thirteen things that can cause anxiety*. Health.com. https://www.health.com/condition/anxiety/things-that-can-cause-anxiety

Nall, R. (2020, September 30). *Panic attack and panic disorder: What you need to know*. Medical News Today. https://www.medicalnewstoday.com/articles/8872

Nall, R. (2022, March 16). *Separation anxiety in adults: Symptoms, treatment, and management*. Medical News Today. https://www.medicalnewstoday.com/articles/322070#causes-in-adults

National Health Service. (2021, February 16). *Panic disorder*. https://www.nhs.uk/mental-health/conditions/panic-disorder/

National Institute of Mental Health. (n.d.). *Teen depression: more than just moodiness*. https://www.nimh.nih.gov/health/publications/teen-depression

National Institute of Mental Health. (2022a). *Major depression*. https://www.nimh.nih.gov/health/statistics/major-depression#part_155721

National Institute of Mental Health. (2022b). *Panic disorder: when fear overwhelms*. https://www.nimh.nih.gov/health/publications/panic-disorder-when-fear-overwhelms

National Institute of Mental Health. (2022c, January). *Major Depression*.

https://www.nimh.nih.gov/health/statistics/major-depression#part_155721

Ng, B. (2018). The neuroscience of growth mindset and intrinsic motivation. *Brain Sciences*, 8(2), 20. https://doi.org/10.3390/brainsci8020020

Nichols, H. (2020, September 29). *Obsessive-compulsive disorder: Symptoms, causes, and treatment.* Medical News Today. https://www.medicalnewstoday.com/articles/178508

NovoPsych. (2021, March 15). *Penn State Worry Questionnaire (PSWQ).* https://novopsych.com.au/assessments/diagnosis/penn-state-worry-questionnaire-pswq/

Olsen, A. (2022, May 19). *The importance of social connection/connectedness for teenage wellbeing.* Komodo Wellbeing. https://www.komodowellbeing.com/wellbeing-resources/the-importance-of-social-connection-connectedness-for-teenage-wellbeing

Osorio, A. (2022, March 24). *Research update: children's anxiety and depression on the rise.* Georgetown University Health Policy Institute. https://ccf.georgetown.edu/2022/03/24/research-update-childrens-anxiety-and-depression-on-the-rise/

Parade. (n.d.). Depression quotes. https://parade.com/946073/parade/depression-quotes/

Parekh, R. (2017). *What are anxiety disorders?* Psychiatry.org. https://www.psychiatry.org/patients-families/anxiety-disorders/what-are-anxiety-disorders

Parkhurst, E. (2021, October 25). *How hobbies improve mental health.* Utah State University. https://extension.usu.edu/mentalhealth/articles/how-hobbies-improve-mental-health

Pedersen, T. (2022, April 22). *The seven best online therapy options for teens for 2022.* Psych Central. https://psychcentral.com/reviews/online-therapy-for-teens

Pietrangelo, A. (2019, December 12). Nine CBT techniques for better mental health. Healthline. https://www.healthline.com/health/cbt-techniques

Princing, M. (2018, July 16). *These at-home cognitive behavioral therapy tips can help ease your anxieties.* Right as Rain by UW Medicine.

https://rightasrain.uwmedicine.org/mind/stress/these-home-cognitive-behavioral-therapy-tips-can-help-ease-your-anxieties

Quist, M. (2022). *Cognitive intervention: Definition and examples.* Study.com. https://study.com/academy/lesson/cognitive-intervention-definition-examples.html

Raypole, C. (2019, September 27). *Thirteen ways to increase endorphins.* Healthline. https://www.healthline.com/health/how-to-increase-endorphins

Raypole, C. (2020, May 27). *Twelve ways to boost oxytocin naturally.* Healthline. https://www.healthline.com/health/how-to-increase-oxytocin

Raypole, C. (2022a, June 13). *Thirty grounding techniques to quiet distressing thoughts.* Healthline. https://www.healthline.com/health/grounding-techniques#mental-techniques

Raypole, C. (2022b, July 26). *How to hack your hormones for a better mood.* Healthline. https://www.healthline.com/health/happy-hormone#sunlight

Raypole, C., & Boyers, L. (2022, February 23). *Eighteen of the best fidget toys for anxiety.* Healthline. https://www.healthline.com/health/fidget-toys-for-anxiety#what-they-are

Raypole, C., & Burford, M. (2022, October 5). *Eleven ways to boost serotonin without medication.* Healthline. https://www.healthline.com/health/how-to-increase-serotonin#exercise

Raypole, C., & Marcin, A. (2022, May 17). *Cognitive behavioral therapy: What is it and how does it work?* Healthline. https://www.healthline.com/health/cognitive-behavioral-therapy#concepts

Rethink Mental Illness. (2021). *What are the signs and symptoms of an anxiety disorder?* https://www.rethink.org/advice-and-information/about-mental-illness/learn-more-about-conditions/anxiety-disorders/

Rice, A. (2022, April 15). *Nearly half of U.S. teens feel sad and hopeless: what can be done?* Psych Central. https://psychcentral.com/news/teenage-mental-health-pandemic-cdc-report

Rowlands, L. (2019, January 25). Why people with anxiety and other mood disorders struggle to manage their emotions. *The Conversation.* https://theconversation.com/why-people-with-anxiety-and-other-mood-disorders-struggle-to-manage-their-emotions-106865

Ruiz, R. (2021, August 9). *Myths about teens with anxiety.* SacWellness. https://sacwellness.com/myths-about-teens-with-anxiety/

Russell, T. (2022, May 24). *Stressors: Recognizing what causes stress.* Forbes Health. https://www.forbes.com/health/mind/what-causes-stress/

Rutter, L. A., Scheuer, L., Vahia, I. V., Forester, B. P., Smoller, J. W., & Germine, L. (2019). Emotion sensitivity and self-reported symptoms of generalized anxiety disorder across the lifespan: A population-based sample approach. *Brain and Behavior, 9*(6). https://doi.org/10.1002/brb3.1282

Salinas, J., O'Donnell, A., Kojis, D. J., Pase, M. P., DeCarli, C., Rentz, D. M., Berkman, L. F., Beiser, A., & Seshadri, S. (2021). Association of social support with brain volume and cognition. *JAMA Network Open, 4*(8). https://doi.org/10.1001/jamanetworkopen.2021.21122

Santos-Longhurst, A. (2022, May 23). *Can coloring really help you relax? Nine reasons to try adult coloring.* Healthline. https://www.healthline.com/health/mental-health/benefits-of-adult-coloring#anxiety-and-depression-relief

Schild, D. (2020, November 4). *Easy hobbies to try that could help make you feel less anxious, from yoga to gardening.* Insider. https://www.insider.com/activities-things-to-do-help-with-stress-anxiety

Schwantes, M. (2017, August 11). *Convince your brain that you are safe.* Inc.Africa. https://incafrica.com/library/marcel-schwantes-6-powerful-brain-hacks-to-cope-with-anxiety-every-

Scott, E. (2020, April 5). Top ten stress-relieving hobbies. Verywell Mind. https://www.verywellmind.com/top-stress-reliever-hobbies-3144592

Scott, E. (2020, November 23). *How to use gardening for stress relief.* Verywell Mind. https://www.verywellmind.com/gardening-for-stress-relief-3144600

Shaikh, J. (2021, June 3). *What is an example of cognitive therapy?*

MedicineNet. https://www.medicinenet.com/what_is_an_example_of_cognitive_therapy/article.htm

Shipman, D. (2016). A prescription for music lessons. *Federal Practitioner, 33*(2), 9–12. https://www.ncbi.nlm.nih.gov/pmc/articles/PMC6368928/

Silva, L. (2022a, August 4). *How to deal with anxiety*. Forbes Health. https://www.forbes.com/health/mind/how-to-deal-with-anxiety/#scrollto_5_ways_to_deal_with_anxiety_section

Silva, L. (2022b, December 1). *The mental health benefits of a clean home*. Forbes Health. https://www.forbes.com/health/mind/mental-health-clean-home/

Sissons, C. (2018, July 10). *Eight foods that boost serotonin naturally*. Medicalnewstoday.com. https://www.medicalnewstoday.com/articles/322416

Sitting Bull. (2023). *A quote by Sitting Bull*. Goodreads. https://www.goodreads.com/quotes/58183-inside-of-me-there-are-two-dogs-one-is-mean

Smith, J. (2020, September 25). *Growth vs fixed mindset: How what you think affects what you achieve*. Mindset Health. https://www.mindsethealth.com/matter/growth-vs-fixed-mindset

Smith, J. (2021, January 17). *Anxiety disorders: symptoms, types, and treatments*. Psych Central. https://psychcentral.com/anxiety/anxiety-disorders#types

Social Media Victims Law Center. (2022). *Effects of cyberbullying: what parents and teenagers need to know*. https://socialmediavictims.org/cyberbullying/effects/

Sparks, S. D. (2021, April 9). "Growth mindset" linked to higher test scores, student well-being in global study. *Education Week*. https://www.edweek.org/leadership/growth-mindset-linked-to-higher-test-scores-student-well-being-in-global-study/2021/04

Stanborough, R. J. (2022, October 25). *What are cognitive distortions and how can you change these thinking patterns?* Healthline. https://www.healthline.com/health/cognitive-distortions

Stanford Medicine Children's Health. (2019). *Major depression in teens*. https://www.stanfordchildrens.org/en/topic/default?id=major-depression-in-adolescents-90-P01614

Star, K. (2020, September 16). *Progressive Muscle Relaxation (PMR) for anxiety*. Verywell Mind. https://www.verywellmind.com/progressive-muscle-relaxation-pmr-2584097

Star, K. (2022, December 12). *How to stop worrying*. Verywell Mind. https://www.verywellmind.com/how-can-i-stop-worrying-so-much-2583982

Tapp, F. (2018, June 27). *Ten anxiety hacks therapists swear by*. HuffPost. https://www.huffpost.com/entry/anxiety-tips-therapists-swear-by_n_5b2bf149e4b00295f15a91bf

Tartakovsky, M. (2021, September 14). *How to Identify the Real Cause of Your Anxiety*. Psych Central. https://psychcentral.com/anxiety/getting-to-the-root-of-your-anxiety

Vandergriendt, C. (2017, November 15). *What's the difference between a panic attack and an anxiety attack?* Healthline. https://www.healthline.com/health/panic-attack-vs-anxiety-attack

Vann, M. R. (2018, August 3). *What it's like to have an anxiety or panic attack*. Everyday Health. https://www.everydayhealth.com/conditions/what-its-like-to-have-an-anxiety-attack/

VanOrman, A. (2022, August 8). Anxiety and depression increase among U.S. youth, 2022 KIDS COUNTS data book shows. *Population Reference Bureau*. https://www.prb.org/resources/anxiety-and-depression-increase-among-u-s-youth-2022-kids-counts-data-book-shows/

Vukelich, L., & Sun, V. (2022, November 2). *The top ten common anxiety triggers you should know about*. CNET. https://www.cnet.com/health/mental/10-common-anxiety-triggers/

Whitten, E. (2014, March 22). *Awake in a nightmare*. HuffPost. https://www.huffpost.com/entry/dealing-with-anxiety_b_4995950

Winstone, L., Mars, B., Haworth, C. M. A., & Kidger, J. (2021). Social media use and social connectedness among adolescents in the United Kingdom: a qualitative exploration of displacement and stimulation. *BMC Public Health*, *21*(1). https://doi.org/10.1186/s12889-021-11802-9

Wisner, W. (2022, March 26). *What to know about PTSD in teenagers*.

Verywell Mind. https://www.verywellmind.com/what-to-know-about-ptsd-in-teenagers-5210244

World Health Organization. (2021, November 17). *Adolescent mental health*. World Health Organization. https://www.who.int/news-room/fact-sheets/detail/adolescent-mental-health

Yapko, M. (2018, April 24). *Why skills can beat pills when it comes to overcoming depression*. Psychlopaedia. https://psychlopaedia.org/health/skills-overcome-pills-to-beat-depression/

Young, K. (2016, February 10). *What you focus on is what becomes powerful - why your thoughts and feelings matter*. Hey Sigmund https://www.heysigmund.com/why-what-you-focus-on-is-what-becomes-powerful-why-your-thoughts-and-feelings-matter/

Made in the USA
Monee, IL
07 December 2023